Teen Zone

Judith Wilson

photography by Winfried Heinze

Teen Zone

STYLISH LIVING FOR TEENS

RYLAND
PETERS
& SMALL

LONDON NEW YORK

Senior designer Megan Smith
Commissioning editor Annabel Morgan
Location research Jess Walton
Production Gordana Simakovic
Art director Anne-Marie Bulat
Publishing director Alison Starling

First published in the United Kingdom in
2007 by Ryland Peters & Small
20–21 Jockey's Fields
London WC1R 4BW
www.rylandpeters.com

10 9 8 7 6 5 4 3 2 1

Text copyright © Judith Wilson 2007
Design and photographs copyright
© Ryland Peters & Small 2007

ISBN-10: 1 84597 350 X
ISBN-13: 978 1 84597 350 6

Contents

As our children grow up and – almost

overnight– turn into mini adults, life at home faces certain upheaval. Areas that were once held sacred after the little ones were in bed, such as a grown-up sitting room, are now likely to be filled with your teenage kids (and their friends). Delightful as this is, for many parents the transition is not altogether welcome. Where can parents go for peace and quiet? Retreat may seem the easiest option, but do you really want to end up in your bedroom watching TV? At a time when parents and teenagers need to keep communication lines open, creating an informal, welcoming environment for the entire family is what really matters, while maintaining privacy for those who need it.

Rearranging existing rooms,

building an extension or moving house are all options, but plan early to get maximum benefit. Remember, too, that this is a time when teens are developing a distinctive style and views of their own. It's important to take that on board. Yes, this is your home, but it is your kids' space too. The more experimental ideas might be better off on trial in teenagers' own rooms, but novel suggestions for shared spaces might surprise you. Don't be sensitive if – horror of horrors – they are critical of your own taste! There's a happy decorative medium, and it's up to everyone to achieve it.

> ' Parenting teenagers makes you a lot more chilled out about things you cared about in the past, such as the sea of towels on the bathroom floor! ' SERA/ MOTHER

With this in mind, *Teen Zone* has been
designed to appeal to parents and kids alike. All the
rooms shown were photographed in real homes.
We've asked parents and teenagers to comment on
what they enjoy about their spaces: you'll find their
quotes throughout the book. The main text is aimed
at parents – because they hold the purse-strings – but
there are special sections written for teens. Get your

kids to check out the Why Don't You… panels for quick, creative ideas,
plus the Hot Topics boxes to get them thinking about shared issues!

So resolve to enjoy this new phase in the life of your
home. Most parents of teenagers will admit to appreciating the need
to creatively rethink spaces at home, relishing the sociable ebb and
flow of kids' friends, and the influx of fresh ideas. The successful
teen-friendly home is all about inclusion, not exclusion. Compromise
is essential. And a balance between the funky and the formal, the
sociable and the private, will achieve the perfect fusion.

Boudoirs for Girls

The teenage years precipitate a powerful search for individuality. Within the family home, your daughter's bedroom is a brilliant place to start: it should be a private place of her own, where she can crystallize her style. Talk to any group of teen girls and the message is clear: they want a space that they can stamp with their own personalities. The colour of the walls or the size of the bed is almost immaterial. What matters most is that your daughter is allowed to exercise control over her room. As a parent, only you can decide on the exact level of privacy. But if you can allow her the small freedom of decorating as she wishes, she will create a space of which she is proud, and in which she will enjoy spending time.

Creating a haven is a vital starting

point. Teenagers are not immune from today's busy world – if anything, coping with school work, relationships and the pressures of growing up makes their lives more complex than our own.

‘I love to change my room around with saris in summer, muslins in winter. It's great to alter the vibe with the seasons. ’

ANOUSHKA/ 16 YRS

'I spend my whole time in here with my friends – they love the seating area. I love my desk because it's so big and cool.'

OLIVE/ 15 YRS

For most kids, the bedroom is, of course, a multifunctional room: a place to entertain friends, to study and to sleep. But with clever planning – from a chill-out seating zone to a special area for scented candles and a tranquil view – it can also become a bolthole from the world. So instil in your daughter the importance of the bedroom as sanctuary. Emphasize it as a positive place to retreat to, rather than as a place to hide away in anger.

Hand over responsibility for the concept and sourcing of the room to your daughter. Suggest she treats it as a school project, with all the research and the planning that this entails. It's much more fun to be in control, especially if you involve her in cost considerations too. Agree on a budget and see if she can stick to it – that way, if she wants to blow most of it on a four-poster bed, she'll need to find a cost-effective option for the walls. Show her how to use a floor plan to get the best out of her bedroom; learning to maximize your living space is one of life's great lessons!

If little girls enjoy their bedrooms, teen girls luxuriate in them even more. In a world where much of their time is spent in communal areas – school, sports clubs, shared spaces at home – they value having a bolthole of their own. Recognize that, and help your daughter to create a special zone. Initiate a definite change, and work with her to put away some (not all) childish things. It is a good idea to do this on the cusp of the teen years, as she moves from primary to secondary school. Alterations in school life, new friends, and an increasing sense of self, all mark a parting of the ways in how she uses her bedroom. It is now a place for study, socializing, preening and relaxing, so deserves a new grown-up look.

Before embarking on a revamp, check if your daughter is happy in her current room. Is there enough space for a decent desk, somewhere to sit with friends? Does its location

Opposite, left Don't hide away groovy vintage and party clothes: show them off by hanging them on a wall or a door. Use a pretty hook, and a satin or faux-fur hanger.
Far left Every girl needs shelves to display treasured possessions: deliberately mix up childhood trinkets, from ballet shoes to favourite dolls, with jewellery and dinky handbags.
Left Pictures tend to create a more sophisticated mood than posters. They don't have to be expensive: a hand–painted watercolour looks good, or a favourite digital photo printed onto canvas.

give her enough privacy? If not, is there the option for her to move to a spare bedroom, away from the parental zone or younger siblings? Moving up to a loft extension may be a possibility. Having a large room isn't necessarily important. Many teen girls prefer a small room because it feels cosy, and they love the romance of an attic space with sloping ceilings. What really matters is that the bedroom be divided into three identifiable zones: sleep, study and entertaining.

It's also important that your daughter's bedroom is literally her own. It can be tempting to store your out-of-season clothes in a child's room. But this can be contentious for kids who want to be in control of their own space. So sort out stray possessions. If they are really important, make space for them in your own room. Or de-clutter and give to charity, along with any toys, children's clothes and treasures your daughter has outgrown. After a clean sweep, there can be no arguments about 'your stuff' being the cause of untidiness.

Long before making decorative decisions, sort out basics like power sources. Are there enough electrical sockets? As well as a computer, mobile phone charger and bedside and desk lamps, what about hair straighteners, the television, stereo speakers, electric guitar and so on? It's hard to stay tidy if there's a muddle of spaghetti wires. Consider the room

Above left Teen girls will appreciate an en suite bath or shower room, however tiny. A sand-blasted glass door gives privacy yet allows for plenty of light flow.
Below left A floor-to-ceiling built-in wardrobe looks streamlined and hides clutter. The upper shelves can be reserved for bulky or rarely used items. Sliding doors maximize space: pick mirrors, opaque glass or coloured laminate rather than wood veneer, which can look boring.
Opposite A built-in desk with storage above is fitted with a sliding panel. When homework is finished, the computer and textbooks can be hidden from view.

WHY DON'T YOU …
>> Go fluffy. The high
street has plenty of funky
cheap cushion covers and
throws in fleece fabric or
fake fur, which are both
cosy to lie on and cool to
look at.
>> Jazz up a boring
rectangular headboard
by reupholstering it with
a couple of metres of fake
fur. Pull the fur tightly
round the headboard and
staple-gun into place.

Left Girly frivolity works best when combined with tongue-in-cheek humour. This silk lampshade looks amazing because it is overscaled and dramatic. To ring the changes between overhead lighting and a bedside lamp, a standard lamp is a good way to introduce extra low-level mood lighting.

Below A plain cupboard door is the perfect place for an ever-changing collage.

Opposite A mixture of vintage bedding and inexpensive fabric panels comes together to create an exotic, feminine bedroom.

layout at the same time, so sockets are in the right place. The addition of a wall-mounted light by the bed will free up a bedside table for other essentials.

Whether your daughter is moving to a new room or revamping her old one, she'll need help with the layout. Stick to the three divisions (sleep, study and socializing) and draw up a floor plan. Try to view the space with fresh eyes. Will a great view from the desk be inspiring, or would concentration come easier if she's facing a blank wall? If the room is tiny, consider dual-purpose built-in furniture, such as a platform bed with a desk beneath. Review the existing furniture. If something is worn out or outgrown, either revamp it or sell it and reinvest the proceeds. Most teen girls will enjoy spray-painting an old chest of drawers silver, or decorating a table with découpage slogans.

Next, focus on the desired decorative mood. Suggest your daughter amass tear sheets from magazines, or sketch her ideas. There are many sources of decorative inspiration: music videos, surf culture or catwalk fashion for starters. Crucially, your daughter's room must reflect her own tastes,

> **'** I love the mirrored door, because when it's shut the room is my own secret hideaway. **'** POLLY/ 17 YRS

Above, left to right A platform bed is still possible even in a tiny room. This low-level design also provides just enough space for a small dressing table.

Left For the tidy-minded only, a wall of shallow open shelves is a great way to organize a groovy collection of shoes and baskets.

Opposite A mirrored door creates an element of surprise: when shut, the entrance to the bedroom is concealed.

not yours. But help her temper her crazier impulses. Instead of all-over Goth rock, one black and one silver wall might suffice; and a boudoir mood is more sophisticated played out in orange and red silk than in lipstick-pink satin.

You can also help by pointing out alternative decorative sources. Suggest she rifles through dress fabric departments (for everything from fake fur to sequinned muslins), visits the local market, and checks out Asian shops (for sari silks) or keeps an eye out for sale bargains or in junk shops (for the odd wacky piece of furniture or lighting). With the rise of digital technology, there is also the option of imposing photographs of, say, a giant leaf or a cityscape onto wallpaper, roller blinds or a duvet cover.

It's a good idea to deliberately stick to a modest budget. If wackily decorated walls can be repainted, ad hoc upholstery ideas rapidly restitched, and cheap furniture swapped around, your daughter will feel more relaxed about experimenting. If a teenager's room is to truly reflect her personality, she must be allowed to customize it and let it evolve over time. So let her choose her own paint colours;

This page Not every girl wants a hippie den: here, bold damask and quilted fabrics add glamour, as do the coordinated cushions and curtains. Experiment with variations on powder-room pink: pale blue, lilac and silver are all glamour-girl alternatives. Cluttered shelves would spoil the look, so wall-to-wall curtains are a great way to conceal inexpensive shelving.
Opposite below Think of finishing touches as the jewellery of the room. Here, tiny cushion tassels make pretty drawer handles. Alternatively, consider glittery coloured glass.

and if she wants navy blue or deepest aubergine, let her, because she has to sleep in there, not you! If your daughter is artistic, get her to invite over her friends, supply multiple paintbrushes, and let them experiment.

Furniture will be your biggest investment. Start with the bed. Sleeping is high on the list of teen activities! By now your daughter will have outgrown her little girl's bed and need an upgrade. If there's no room for a separate sofa, choose a plain divan without a headboard to double as a daybed, which can be layered with velvet or satin throws. Alternatively, get an upholsterer to make a fitted cover in an inexpensive cotton twill. Your daughter can customize it with bold embroidery and quotes written in fabric pen, or by trimming the edges with beads or ribbon.

WHY DON'T YOU …
>> Add sparkle. A garland of funky flower-shaped lights or white tree lights wound around your headboard or dressing-table mirror will give off an atmospheric night-time glow.
>> Beg or buy a few faceted antique glass droplets from a chandelier shop, or dig out twinky faux-crystal Christmas tree decorations, then suspend them on invisible thread (or pretty ribbon) from the ceiling to catch the sunshine.

HOT TOPICS/ ORGANIZATION

Keeping the bedroom tidy may require compromise: your view of organized may not match your parents'. But finding files, clothes and favourite things is easier if everything has a special place. Efficient storage, and plenty of it, is the answer. Even if your room is tiny, you can still be organized. Great storage extras are under-bed drawers on wheels (brilliant for private stuff you don't want on display), shallow wall shelves (for CDs, books, files and treasures), and a second-hand filing cabinet (for notes, computer printouts and catalogues). For organizing things like shoes, a giant wicker or plastic linen basket by the door is an excellent idea. Have a once-weekly or once-monthly tidy-up, and everyone will be happy.

In a small room, choose furniture that offers space-saving solutions, such as a built-in platform bed. The space beneath can be used as a study area or sitting zone. The platform should be high enough so things don't get cramped down below and, if ceiling height allows, it is a good idea to situate the bed immediately above the door, freeing up space for a desk and seating. If you have a bed custom-built, you can choose the method of access – a conventional ladder, steel rungs on the wall, painted MDF 'steps' (which can double as storage) or a fireman's pole. In a room with restricted ceiling height, create a lower-height built-in bed, with drawers below, and an oval opening to create a trendy 'pod' design.

Every girl deserves a quiet, well-organized space for studying. Some girls are distracted when working in their bedrooms, while others can't relax with a direct view of unfinished homework. So try to create a formal division between bed and desk. One solution is to design an extra-deep built-in cupboard, which hides the desk and shelves

If there is the space to make the bed a focus in the room, choose an unusual design. For emergent punks, a second-hand cast-iron bedstead is excellent, particularly if slightly scuffed and painted black. More romantic teens will enjoy a metal or wood four-poster, which can be endlessly reinvented with different fabrics, from cherry taffeta panels to white muslin. A wall-mounted corona is also a cool option. Dress it with multicoloured netting or strings of glass beads. Many girls will ask for a double bed – a thorny issue for some parents. The benefits are manifold – there's plenty of room for friends to lounge, it's a cosy place to hunker down, and – once kids have left home – it becomes a useful spare bed. Who your daughter chooses to share it with is an issue for you and your daughter alone! This is a good time to invest in a new mattress – teenagers need one with firm support.

Opposite For an edgier mood, an eclectic mix of junk-shop furniture, random posters and muted colours sets the tone. But even industrial style needs to be comfy, too, so layer a metal bedstead with cosy blankets and soft pillows.
Above left Having a small table and chairs is useful when friends come over, and can double as a study zone.
Right Favourite toys can still look funky if mixed with grown-up accessories.

behind closed doors. In a larger, modern room, a sliding MDF door can partition off the study area from the sleeping zone, or fit a suspension wire to the ceiling and use fabric panels. Even a conventional three-panel screen, decorated with a montage of magazine images, provides a clever division.

The most useful desk is long and deep, so there's room for a computer, textbooks and papers. The cheapest solution is to fit a length of chunky MDF along one wall, with space below for filing cabinets and a desk chair. It can also double as a dressing table. Leave your daughter to decorate the tabletop – painting it in a funky colour, or covering it with a

Left and far left Take time to pick different ways of creating ambience: incense sticks and candles are traditional cheap-and-cheerful teen favourites.
Below left There are some fabulously trendy wallpaper designs featuring graphic prints that work well in a teenage girl's room.
Opposite Allocate a large section of wall to an evolving collage of photos, magazine images and other odds and ends. A metal pinboard with magnets is best if the walls are wallpapered, or, if one wall is painted a plain colour, use Blu-tack. The display can become an artwork in its own right, frequently edited and added to for a good mix of pattern and colour.

WHY DON'T YOU …

>> Make your own cushion covers with remnants of funky dress fabrics, from leather to lace, or raid market stalls for vintage silk scarves to stitch together.

>> Customize! A plain upholstered armchair or curtains will look amazing randomly adorned with odd buttons, lengths of ribbon or junk jewellery.

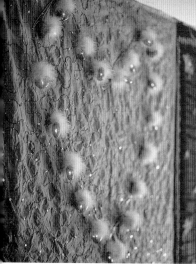

Left and below Properly done, a painted wall devoted to doodles, autographs and poems from friends can look fantastic. Keep permanent markers in a choice of colours, so the wall can be added to at any time.
Opposite above left Fabric panels such as sari silks in vibrant shades are a cheap, cheerful way to add colour to plain walls, and can be changed every few months.
Opposite above right A vintage desk in metal provides a decorative focus, as well as plenty of storage.
Opposite below right A rug is cosy on painted floorboards and comfortable for lounging on the floor.

collage of bus tickets. A trestle table is also inexpensive. A glass top looks sophisticated, or opt for a plywood top then use a staple gun to cover it with oilcloth or artist's canvas (great fun to doodle on). An adjustable-height chair on castors with proper lumbar support is important. Provide your daughter with a second-hand office chair, a needle and a basket of remnants, and let her customize that too.

Every child has files and textbooks to store, so help your daughter to create an organized storage system. The easiest solution is a deep shelf running the length of the desk. A free-standing industrial-style metal shelf unit also looks good. If your daughter wants a prettier option, ask her to draw a decorative template and get a carpenter to cut out

28

HOT TOPICS/ NOISE

Noise is always going to be an issue in a busy home. Either you're accused of making too much, such as playing music, or everyone else's noise disturbs you when you're studying. Extra insulation between two rooms will be achieved by lining the dividing wall with built-in cupboards (preferably in both rooms). Or cover an entire wall with cork tiles: they are inexpensive, insulate against noise and provide a dramatic area for display. More importantly, come to a family agreement on noise. If you need to study, add a white board on your door that delivers a 'Quiet, Please' message. When friends are over, agree a curfew time, after which low music and voices are the acceptable level.

Above left However tiny, a separate seating area in the bedroom is sociable. Friends can chill out here, and kids have somewhere separate to relax when studying is over. In this room, a low daybed with lots of cushions is just as comfy as a sofa. Add a coffee table if possible, for candles and drinks. The table needn't be expensive. A square of MDF can be painted, randomly tiled or stuck with a mosaic of shells or stones collected on the beach.

Above and below right Customizing paintwork with graffiti-style motifs is fun to do and looks individual. It is most effective if contained within a specific area, such as a door or the sides of shelves.

Opposite For a funky, moody look, use deep, warm colours on every surface, and leave the plain white paint for the rest of the house.

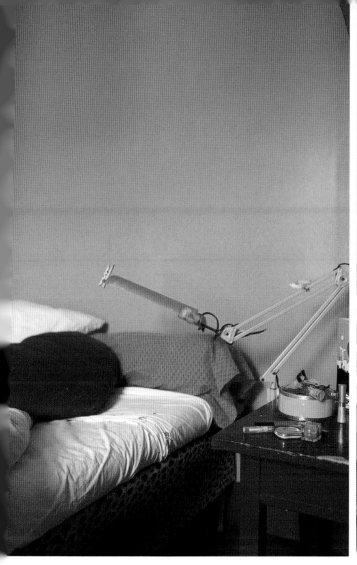

curvy edges to jazz up wall-mounted shelves. Existing shelves can be edged with ribbon trims or narrow painted picture mouldings. Wall-mounted metal magazine holders are an excellent way to organize papers.

Proper clothes storage is essential. If there's a place for everything, there's no excuse for a floor littered with shoes and tops. She'll need full-length hanging space combined with drawers or open shelves for folded tops and underwear, and hooks for sports kit and bags. Built-in floor-to-ceiling cupboards along one wall are the best solution, fitted with wire baskets, rails and hooks. Customize panelled doors using chicken wire lined with fabric, or remove them entirely and hang velvet or muslin curtains in their place. In a tiny room, mirror panels on doors will create a sense of space. On plain doors, use stick-on mouldings to create panels, then let your daughter fill them with a montage of images.

Don't overlook the extras that allow for a bit of preening. Every girl needs a full-length mirror: in a modern room, mirror the back of the door, or look out for an inexpensive mirror with an extravagantly moulded frame, then paint over cheap gilt with black, silver or funky lime green. A dressing table is a brilliant place to hold the inevitable clutter of make up, jewellery, perfume and personal ephemera. If your daughter likes a vintage look, search for a retro-style kidney-shaped dressing table with matching pouffe or, for a sleek finish, wall-mount a deep shelf and tuck a stool below.

Crash Pads for Boys

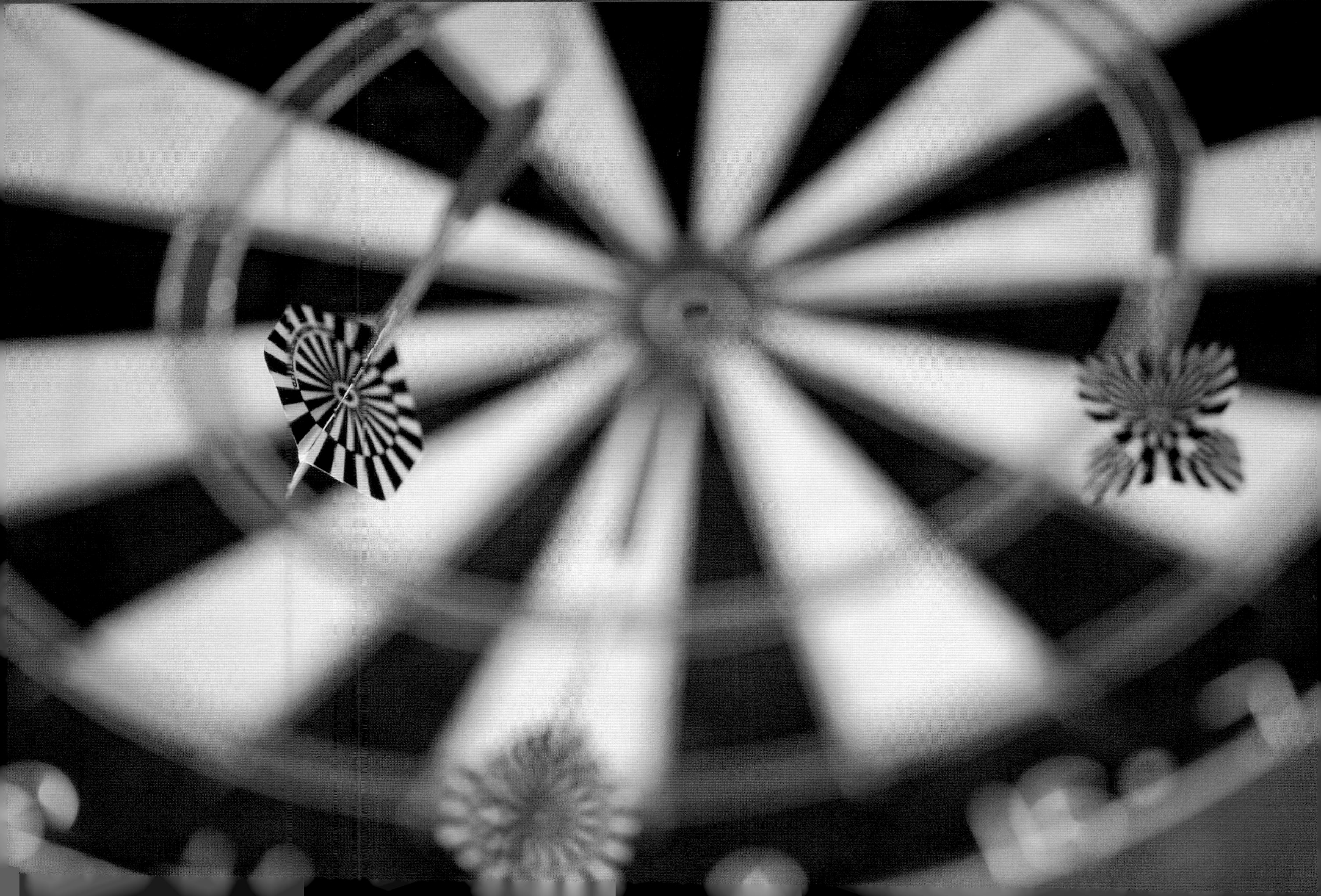

Teen boys want cool rooms too

Their bedrooms should be a space where they can study, sleep, hang out with friends and relax, but also be a show-off zone for their passions. Just because a teenage boy's room is assumed to be a no-go area filled with smelly trainers doesn't mean your son's has to be the same. If you are enthusiastic and proactive about creating a well-planned room and inspired decor, he will be too. By the teenage years, your son will know exactly what look he wants to achieve. Whether that's no-nonsense and functional, clutter-filled and cheery, or moodily atmospheric, he will most likely need your creative input (and money!) to turn his initial ideas into a finished space.

Creative freedom – be that painting

the floorboards black or covering the walls with maps – is one thing, but the issue of privacy is another. From the moment an older boy gets a computer and/or a TV in the bedroom (and the

'I think your room represents who you are and reflects your personality. That's why mine is so cool.'

FREDDIE/ 15 YRS

34

'I like my room because of the great colour
I chose, the size, the large windows and the TV.
All my friends love coming over.'

HARRY / 13 YRS

unlimited access that this inevitably brings), there
will always be issues about how much time he
spends in his room, and how much parental control
you can exercise. Installing software to screen
unsuitable material helps, as does an agreement
about time spent on the computer. More positively,
persuade him to make the room sociable, so that he
can make you and the rest of the family feel welcome
(if invited!). Putting the computer in a visible spot also helps.

Functionality is crucial in a teen boy's room. Storage
should be easy to access, technology sorted, and surfaces robust. Ask
your son if there are particular styles of furniture or gadgets that he
thinks are cool. These might range from big ideas, like a vintage
leather armchair (in which case he might want to start saving), to
small ones, like having a kettle in his room for greater independence.
Encourage him to take responsibility for his space, including keeping
it reasonably neat. That way you don't have to nag and he's more
likely to chuck clothes in the laundry bin and make his bed

Left the bedroom door is a potent symbol of a teenager's privacy as well as marking the entrance to a boy's independent zone. In a relaxed household, it can be fun to decorate the door with stickers and logos. Alternatively, consider a more formal decorative option: paint the door a funky colour, or fit it with a porthole-style round window.

Opposite A simple mural is a brilliant way to set a decorative theme. Print out a digital photo of a graphic image, mark it (and the walls) up into a grid, then hand-paint the image, section by section, onto the wall. Get some friends along to help.

Personalize a passion. Teen boys will find it easier to create a distinctive look inspired by a favourite activity, from surfing to music, rather than conventionally picking colours or wallpapers. Suggest he downloads or photographs his favourite images, graphics, icons or logos and uses them as a starting point.

It's a myth that teenage boys don't care about their bedrooms. But they do have a different take on them to girls. Pattern, luxurious texture and the display of beautiful things don't matter: the presence of all the correct 'kit' – be that computers, guitars or a sound system – certainly does. If that is hard to get your head around, think of the way teenagers dress. Girls will concentrate on fashionable details, as well as overall image, while boys want something that looks sharp, can be shrugged on and then forgotten. The same applies to the bedroom. The look and layout concern them, but it's the stuff that's in there that really matters.

This page A simple scheme with white walls and dark carpet is enlivened by a creative choice of lighting – a groovy 1960s-style pendant. Other funky choices include pendants with a mirror finish, coloured acrylic shades, or giant paper drum shapes with a laser-cut pattern. Adding a coloured light bulb creates a moody ambience.

Right Robust fittings, such as a chunky radiator or a ceiling fan for ventilation, can be functional and smart.

Below If displays of naked ladies are inevitable, at least show them off in a tongue-in-cheek manner. This hand-painted mural, with paint swirling around magazine cuttings, looks visually pleasing, and – when viewed from a distance – will spare a visitor's blushes.

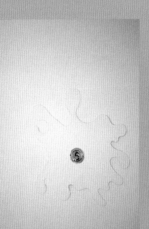

Finding the right location at home for a boy's room is just as crucial as it is for girls. You will probably prefer some physical distance between your son's room and your own bedroom, and so will he. The inevitable noise won't bother you so much, and he will retain a sense of privacy. If a loft or basement conversion is planned, then this can be the ideal time to move him up- or downstairs. Some boys will jump at the chance of a ground floor or even a basement room. They won't be bothered by the lack of daylight, and late-night homecomings will be less of an issue for everyone. If he's moving to another room, is there a chance of providing a small en suite shower room? Many boys will be surprisingly enthused by the possibility.

HOT TOPICS/ TASTE

The second you have opinions of your own, it's a fact that your parents won't necessarily agree. Take a pragmatic view: you don't have to concur on everything. You may hate their music, and they may loathe yours. But it's great if you all enjoy the way your home looks. Instead of criticizing your parents' taste, make creative suggestions. Collect photos or magazine cuttings of interesting decorative ideas and suggest how they could work at home. Areas such as the hall, a TV den or the kitchen are the best places for a mix of the groovy and the unexpected. Here, a jumbled display of toy pistols hanging above the banisters looks just as good as a piece of modern art.

Below A swivel chair looks smart and is the best choice for a homework desk. Choose one with low arms, so it can be pulled comfortably up to the table. There are plenty of colourful and trendy office chairs on the high street.

Right It can be fun to layer a plain cotton duvet and pillowcases with a warm faux-fur animal skin, plaid blanket or fleece throw. Get a big one, so that when friends come over it can be tossed over the entire bed.

Far right Take a look at favourite sportswear or team logos and interpret them as a decorative motif. In this room, the New York Yankees monogram has been hand-painted to define and decorate one wall.

Decoratively speaking, it may be up to you to jump-start your son into action. Inventive surfaces for walls and floors make a great starting point. Most teen boys will welcome an edgy, urban look, and the inevitable raw surfaces are supremely practical. If building work is in progress, consider removing plaster and leaving the brickwork exposed on one wall. This looks great teamed with intense colours like purple or scarlet. Polished plaster walls are expensive but look cool, or sealed render is cheaper. Walls can be lined with natural materials that also have the benefit of extra insulation. Tongue-and-groove boards can be painted in a dark colour like graphite or khaki, or use one-metre squares of plywood nailed onto the wall and varnished. Cork tiles are cheap: use them to create a wall-size pinboard.

The thought of dozens of pairs of huge trainers collecting on your son's bedroom floor will help you make sensible flooring choices. Don't spend a fortune. A plain carpet in a neutral tone teamed with a funky faux animal-skin rug is ideal. Contract cord carpet is robust and comes in many colours, or try carpet tiles. A hard floor is sensible.

Provided floorboards have been sanded and sealed, the cheapest option is to get your son to paint his floor in a plain colour (or get creative with camouflage patterns, stripes or graffiti). Rubber tiles come in great colours, or there are vinyl tiles in wood, stone or water effects. For the ultimate urban look, choose stainless-steel panels or lay reclaimed flooring from an architectural salvage yard.

Choosing good-looking hardware, including radiators, door handles and cupboard knobs, is an inventive way to set a no-nonsense, practical style. If the rest of the room has deliberately plain built-in cupboards and utility-style furniture, investing in a tubular steel radiator and chunky stainless-steel handles is definitely worthwhile. Get your son

Above left For those who take music seriously, siblings (or parents) can be prevented from fiddling with your equipment by allocating a corner for instruments and amplifiers, with other things stored properly on stands. A rock theme is fun to interpret decoratively. Classic photos look smart in identical frames, but for a chill-out den, overlap rock concert posters across an entire wall.

Above right Deep drawers are a useful way to organize CDs and computer games.
Opposite above Create a more sophisticated tailored look with interesting textures and clever detailing. This college-age boy's room has hessian-lined walls and a studded headboard.
Opposite below Vintage furniture adds character, and reclamation stores make fruitful hunting grounds.

to research different styles on the internet, then go with him to a reclamation centre or a hardware store to look and feel the options. He'll find this much more interesting than being dragged around a wallpaper showroom.

Not all boys want an edgy urban look: the artistically minded may want to experiment with colour and texture. Try to allow your son the freedom to try out good ideas. However, it's fair enough to ask that he present you with a sketch or mood board explaining his vision before spending any cash. If he wants to spray-paint graffiti, insist that it is done on a small portion of wall first, so that you are both happy with the results. A graphic display of objects stuck

> ❛ My room is so cool. I love my bed and the space is perfect for just hanging with my friends. ❜
>
> **TATE/ 18 YRS**

onto the wall can also look fantastic; anything from beer bottle tops to skateboards. Alternatively, ask him to create a display on a giant canvas, or a large piece of plywood, so that the bedroom walls remain intact. Decorating a bedroom around a theme, perhaps inspired by a passion for rock music, sport or surf culture, is another brilliant starting point.

Get the power sources sorted early on. As well as a bedside light and desk lamp to plug in, there may be a TV, gaming consoles, DVD, computer(s) and assorted stereos, not to mention an electric guitar, amplifier or mixing desks, if he's into music. If there are several computers in the family home, this could be the right time to go wireless. To house the television, it's worthwhile buying a mobile media unit or

trolley, so that all the kit is together. High-street stores have inexpensive but good-looking metal versions. If space is tight, wall-mount a small TV on an extendable arm.

A teenager's bedroom has to be multi-functional, so pick flexible lighting for a variety of tasks. As well as decent overhead lighting, either from a central pendant or a low voltage source, your son will need a powerful task light for studying. We've all become accustomed to lighting as a mood-inducing tool. High-street lighting is inventive and inexpensive, so treat your son to two or three groovy light sources. LED light coils, a lava lamp, a wall-mounted neon sign or a 'curtain' light all look fantastic. Don't throw up your hands in horror if he prefers an unadorned light bulb: several hanging in a line can look really cool.

Above They may no longer be played with, but a great collection of toy cars, especially vintage ones, make for an eye-catching display.
Right Sports trophies, from signed balls to caps with logos, deserve to be on display. Smaller items can be displayed in a wall-mounted glass-fronted case.
Opposite A busy room can still look orderly if everything has a home and open shelves are regularly tidied.

WHY DON'T YOU...
>> Mix a paint colour that's totally unique to your bedroom. You'll need a plastic painter's bucket, a pale and a dark version of your basic colour (e.g. khaki or grey), and white paint. Now get mixing!
>> It's fun and unusual to paint one wall in a graded colour. As you're painting the wall, keep adding more white to your paint colour, so that the shade lightens.

Given the amount teenagers like to sleep, don't overlook the importance of light control. Keep things simple. A blackout roller blind in black or white, Venetian blinds in metal or wood, or American style shutters are functional and provide privacy. Where full-length curtains are appropriate, a simple, gathered drape in black velvet, hessian, denim or calico, with a tie-top or giant eyelet heading, is the best choice. Hang curtains on a plain steel or wooden pole. For an older boy who likes a tailored look, use pinstripe, tartan or tweeds.

Your son may be a skinny thirteen-year-old now, but teenage boys rapidly morph into gangly giants. If you want to encourage your son to hang out at home with his friends (as opposed to being unsupervised somewhere else), choose welcoming furniture for his room. Teen boys enjoy chilling out together, so plan a layout that caters for sociable gatherings. They won't care particularly about smart furniture, but sufficient space does matter.

So, start with the bed. If space is tight, choose a bed that's low to the ground, so it doubles as a seating area. Pick either a divan on wheels or a Japanese-style platform bed, which provides plenty of room for perching around the mattress itself. A platform bed, accessed via a ladder, leaves space underneath for beanbags or floor cushions. It's always worth having a mattress for friends to crash on. Dual-purpose seating, such as a cube that converts into a single bed, or a futon-style chair, is a great investment. A hammock is also fun. If space allows, add armchairs or even a sofa. Upholstery should be gently distressed – try cracked leather, dark velvet or chunky jumbo cord brightened with a few giant patchwork pieces. A vintage tub chair looks trendy.

A good desk, with a comfortable height-adjustable swivel chair, is essential. It's possible to get a great variety of smartly designed, inexpensive desk styles, from copies of twentieth-century classics to funky coloured melamine, glass or wood veneer tabletops teamed with metal or wood legs. Trestle styles have room below for a filing cabinet. American-style 1950s metal desks are a good option, as they have lots of deep drawers. If the computer is to sit on the desk, remember that several friends may want to gather around the monitor. A narrow dining table, or a length of painted MDF, makes a spacious option. Tabletops should withstand wear and tear. A stainless-steel or zinc top, a junk-shop scrubbed pine table or an old workbench are good choices.

Teen boys aren't renowned for keeping their clothes immaculate, but if you provide them with a simple, user-friendly storage system they may pleasantly surprise you. Hanging space for school uniform, jackets and shirts is essential: a built-in cupboard can be fitted into even the narrowest alcove using double-height hanging rails. A floor-to-ceiling set of deep shelves, either open or within a cupboard, will hold jeans, T-shirts and everything else.

Opposite above For a crisp, smart look, mix natural textures and primary colours. This bedroom has been carefully planned to cater for three distinct activities. The bed is tucked below the window, the desk takes centre stage, and there is a daybed on the opposite wall.
Opposite below Wall-mounted storage is the best way to keep track of stuff that is in daily use. A hanging plastic organizer like this one is home to disks, photos and school information.
Above Classic illustrations from *Tintin* or *The Simpsons* are so good they deserve to framed properly rather than just stuck on the wall as posters. It can be fun to preserve images that were enjoyed as a child and to rework them in a teen bedroom with a more sophisticated treatment.

HOT TOPICS/ PRIVACY

Everyone is entitled to privacy at home. If your bedroom door is shut, your parents, siblings and friends should get in the habit of knocking (and waiting for an answer!) before coming in. But if you keep your door shut the whole time, it can give out a really unwelcoming (and unfriendly) vibe. Come up with a system to let people know when they can, or can't, come for a chat. Design a hotel-style 'Do Not Disturb' sign to hang on the door when you need some privacy, or use a school metalwork class to laser-cut a sign with a phrase like 'Quiet, Please'. Alternatively, take a tip from recording studios, and rig up a light above the door with a green or a red bulb to signal whether or not you're free.

Left A built-in desk with shallow shelves above keeps everything looking neat in a small bedroom.

Above It's simple to custom-make stencils – often it's possible to use the art facilities at school. Choose something simple, like a favourite word or logo.

Right Posters look fabulous used en masse; provided Blu-tack is used, the display can be changed frequently. To create a bold collage effect, photocopy digital photos onto large sheets of paper.

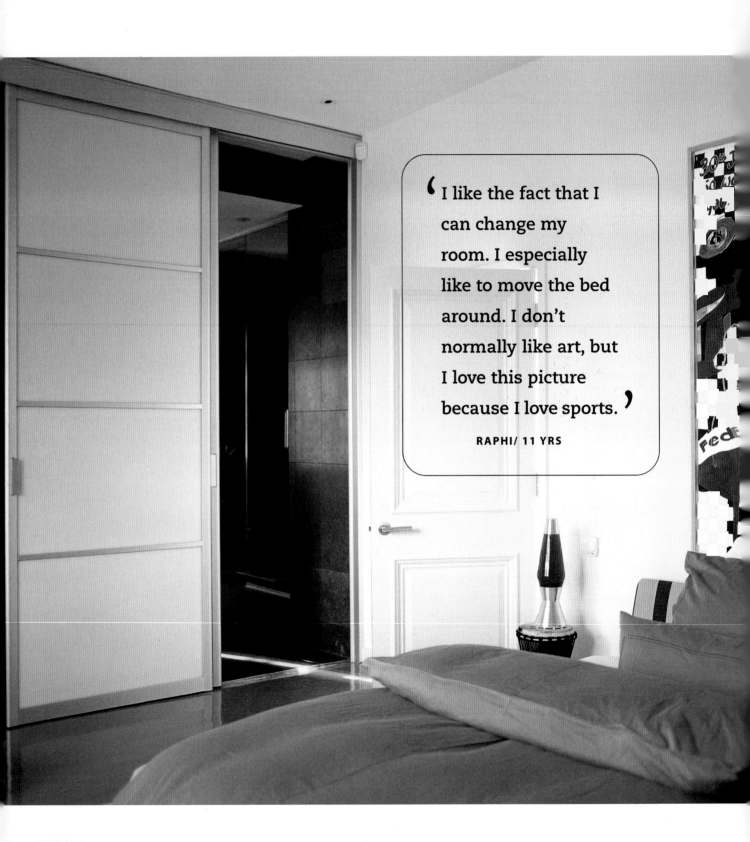

'I like the fact that I can change my room. I especially like to move the bed around. I don't normally like art, but I love this picture because I love sports.'

RAPHI/ 11 YRS

Left and right If space (and budget) allows, an en suite shower room is a great addition to a teen boy's room. Here, the entrance is adjacent to a wall of built-in cupboards (see right): sliding doors conceal clutter when they are shut. For older boys, a slick modern design can work better than a raw urban look, and is still appropriate for visits once they've left home. If surfaces and walls are plain, add one giant visual image to create interest.

Japanese-style sliding screens or roll-up canvas panels are a smart alternative to cupboard doors, and a factory-style metal locker is brilliant for sports equipment. Fit large hooks on the wall, so jeans can be casually hung up in a line. Shoes can be tossed into a giant basket or rubber bucket.

As an alternative to the computer and TV, most teen boys will appreciate the addition of a pub-style game. A dartboard takes up minimal space and looks graphic on the wall; a basketball hoop above a door is very therapeutic for moments when study gets too much. If there's room, table football is a good extra. Teen boys may also enjoy resurrecting treasures from their parents' youth: a record turntable with a collection of 1970s LPs is newly cool.

Some boys can survive happily without a single treasure or decorative object in sight, while others take great pride in displaying signed sports photos, vintage cars or trophies. In a small room, a shallow shelf running around the perimeter of the room can hold the latest team photos, or fit a wall of modular shelving to store books, CDs and DVDs. A pinboard in cork or metal (complete with magnets) is a great space for showing off photos, concert tickets and memorabilia. Ask your son to focus on what he loves best. If he is reluctant to show off his possessions, point out to him that it is the personal ephemera that makes someone's room interesting. It's his space, so he should show off the things that make him feel proud.

WHY DON'T YOU...
>> D-I-Y art. Ask the most artistic person in your class to paint an artist's canvas in whatever medium they like. They will be flattered!
>> Experiment with photography. Spend a day taking photos of your local environment, be that green trees, manhole covers, or neon signs and street lights. Then get your local photo shop to print the best image onto a large canvas that you can hang on the wall.

As kids get older, family bathrooms need
to change. Small children happy to splash then dash turn into big girls and boys who occupy the bathroom for hours on end. On weekdays, when school and sports dominate, they may also want once- or twice-daily showers, all – it seems – at exactly the same time. So rethinking your wash facilities is a smart idea. In an ideal world, as parents, you may wish to have your own en suite bath or shower room so kids can have their own facilities. Or is now the right time to upgrade what was once a children's bathroom into a cool shower room teenagers will appreciate? Kids these days tend to be very well groomed, so giving them a space of their own isn't so much a luxury as a necessity.

Creating a new bathroom or
shower needn't break the bank: it is usually the luxurious textures and designer sanitary ware that ups the cost of a new bathroom. Work out a budget you can afford, and stick to it. There are

**' My bedroom is my haven. It also has a pink
en suite bathroom – what EVERY girl needs! '**

PHOEBE/ 17 YRS

> ' It's great that we have our own bathroom because it's like having a suite, although guests tend to use it as well. '
>
> **DANIELA/ 13 YRS**

often bargains to be had in bathroom and tile showrooms: end-of-line stock, odd pieces from a matching suite or dwindling stocks of a particular tile design. Often, a mix-and-match approach can result in a more enterprising design. Teenagers won't care whether flooring is marble or vinyl: what does matter is that the room functions efficiently. Plentiful hot water and a huge mirror will be top of the list.

Agree firm house rules on tidying up the bathroom so

it's ready for the next user. If kids have difficulty remembering, get a hotel-style sign made and fix it to the door. At the very least, ask for towels to be hung up, the bath or shower and basin to be wiped down after use and the myriad bath and beauty products kept in reasonable order. In many households, the kids' bathroom is also the guest bathroom, so this is doubly important. Make sure there is a giant wash basket for dirty clothes, and insist that it is used. If space permits, you could even install a washing machine and tumble-dryer; then they can take responsibility for their own washing.

Keep things simple. In a shared family bathroom that must cater for teenagers, parents and visitors alike, the space should be streamlined, the decor simple (and preferably monochrome), and the facilities, from plumbing to lighting, faultless. To ensure privacy, consider allocating one bathroom cabinet or basket to each family member.

Choosing the right size and location for teen washrooms is the first task. If your house is sufficiently large, each teenager will enjoy a small en suite shower room off their bedroom. If a bedroom is big enough, a 'slice' of the room could be partitioned off with a new stud wall to create an internal washroom behind. Alternatively, a spare bedroom adjacent to a teen room can be plumbed and turned into a bathroom. Can bedrooms be arranged so that a small washroom sits between two bedrooms, to be shared by siblings? If you are moving house, or doing building work, try to plan for an extra bathroom. Even if you're adapting existing accommodation, the expense of installing a new bathroom is a real investment.

For parents who have their own en suite facilities, it makes sense to revamp the family bathroom to suit teenagers. Does the sanitary ware work well for older kids? A tiny, low-level basin and a bath installed a decade ago might be better replaced by twin basins and a power shower. Ask your children what they prefer: quick showers or a relaxing bath? Alternatively, if

Opposite This cleverly planned family bathroom has a giant bathtub for relaxing, with a shower tucked behind the central wall. Utility-style surfaces appeal to trendy teens and sophisticated parents alike.

Far left Open shelving is often the best solution in a family bathroom. Here, the space below the countertop holds wicker baskets, sponge bags and other supplies.

Left If space is tight, a walk-in shower is a good option, as space is not required for a door to open and shut. A wall-mounted towel rail at one end warms the space.

HOT TOPICS/ BEING GREEN
Your parents may not be quite so eco-minded as you are, so
you might want to tell them a few key water-saving facts.
A five-minute shower uses approximately 35 litres of water,
while a bath uses a whopping 80 to 100 litres. If they can't
decide whether to invest in a new bathroom or shower, this
could be a deciding factor. It's also possible to fit a shower
restrictor that limits the amount of water that flows from the
showerhead. If they are going to add a new WC, they should
choose a dual-flush loo or one with a water-saving cistern.
Any existing loos can become more 'green' if they're fitted
with a cistern device that reduces the flush volume.

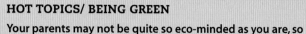

you don't want to spend money changing the fittings, consider whether an extra shower and
loo might be installed elsewhere. Is there space in a downstairs utility room, or an unused
alcove under the stairs? A shower and loo can be fitted into a surprisingly small space.

A tiny washroom calls for inventive solutions. In a wide room with little depth, arrange all
facilities along one wall; the WC and shower contained within two separate 'cubicles' with a
basin and mirror tucked in between the two. A wetroom-style shower, with a wall-mounted
basin and a loo, also works well in a small space. If there isn't enough room for a full-size bath,
fit a shower instead. Don't try to compromise – teenage boys won't enjoy squeezing into a
sitz bath. But do check out specialist ranges by bathroom manufacturers designed for tiny
bathrooms. These days there are some very inventive options to be found.

Opposite left Every centimetre counts in this loft bathroom. Choosing the right style of basin can help: a design with a broad, flat surround like this is great for holding toiletries. A wall-mounted style leaves space below the basin for a magazine rack or a stack of boxes to hold towels or other essential supplies.

Opposite right Think of space-saving ways to connect an en suite bathroom and bedroom. Folding plywood doors (as shown here) or sliding sand-blasted glass or MDF panels are all good options.

This page Plain paint in a fun colour is an inexpensive way to add a funky touch to plain white sanitary ware.

> ' This is very much a vacation house: the colours in the bathroom are bright, to give energy and to provide luminosity. ' LUC/ FATHER

The addition of an extra washroom puts pressure on the hot-water supplies, so it's a good idea to get a plumber to assess whether your hot water tank is up to the task. This may be the time to add a new tank, so that there are no arguments about who has, or hasn't, had a hot shower. At the same time, think about bathroom heating. Invest in a wall-mounted heated towel rail; either one with a built-in radiator panel or a large one that pumps out enough heat to warm the room. Teenagers get through a lot of towels, so a decent heated towel rail is well worth the investment.

A large bathroom means space for both a bath and a separate shower. Think about the layout. If it's possible to screen the shower from the bath, then two girls or two boys

Opposite above left A little imagination can make bathroom facilities more interesting. Here, a simple WC has been given character by adding a canopy on wheels. Commercial-style fittings, such as a stainless-steel loo-roll holder, are witty touches.

Opposite below left With its floor drain and loo cubicle, this neat shower room is very practical, but the coloured tiles add a trendy detail.

Opposite above right By fixing a bowl-style basin onto a table, a bathroom corner is transformed into a dressing area. A big mirror is essential.

Above left A plain but brightly coloured surface, such as laminate, can create a very individual look: laminate is durable and comes in many colours and finishes.

Above right Mix open shelves with a cupboard or two for stashing medicines.

may not mind using the room at the same time. One solution is to fit the bath against a full-height partition wall, with a walk-in shower concealed behind it. Alternatively, place the bath in the centre of the room, with a free-standing screen round it, and the shower in a corner. This is a sociable arrangement but maintains privacy. Twin wash basins, either wall-mounted side by side, or two vanity units, each one on an opposite wall, speed up the morning rush.

Decoratively speaking, it's possible to create a brightly coloured, funky bathroom without breaking the bank. A budget way to introduce colour is to use mosaic or plain tiles. Tiling the inside of a shower or splashbacks in scarlet or swimming-pool blue will cheer up plain white sanitary ware.

This page If there is just one bathroom for the whole family, then choose a more sophisticated style with trendy detailing. Here, the double-ended curved bath and soothing scheme pleases parents, while the walk-in shower suits teens in a hurry

WHY DON'T YOU...
>> Ask for colour-coded towels for each member of the family. The boys can have grey, navy, aubergine or chocolate, while the girls can have hot pink and orange tones. You'll soon be able to tell who hasn't hung up their towels!
>> Add atmosphere for relaxing bathtimes. Add one giant scented candle or choose lots of tea lights to set around the bath.

> ' The hallway to my room leads to my own bathroom and closet, so it feels like a mini apartment. '
>
> **GIBSON/ 13 YRS**

Shell pink, lilac or powder blue are great for a girl's retro-style bathroom, or use black or white metro-style tiles in a boy's washroom. Use tiles to create patterns. Mosaic tiles can be used to create bands in a contrast shade, or pick out a bold, graphic pattern with larger tiles.

Design-conscious teenagers will also enjoy more unusual finishes. Polished plaster walls, or one wall clad with stainless-steel or varnished plywood panels are all comparatively inexpensive options. Investigate textured floor tiles, from slate to pebble-texture varieties. Some are also suitable for use on the walls, and can create a groovy all-over design. Fun options for floors include patterned vinyl, rubber or lino.

There is such a tempting range of colourful, design-led choices for bathrooms these days that it's a shame not to choose one amazing piece to provide a focus and team it with budget fittings elsewhere. You could mix cheap white sanitary ware with a sheet laminate wall in a zingy colour like lemon or tangerine. Many bathroom manufacturers now produce brightly coloured basins: a green bowl teamed with black-tiled surfaces will look funky. Or include a custom-made piece of glass or laminate. Digital photography techniques are now so sophisticated that it's possible to have any image, from a seascape to green leaves, printed onto glass to create a splashback or a shower door.

Above left and above
Where space is tight, a wall-mounted basin is the best option: there are also corner-mounted options for a really small room. It's worth visiting a reclamation centre for unusual, one-off vintage fittings to add character: these can look dramatic teamed with a modern spout or wall-mounted tap.

Left In a family bathroom, keep plenty of spare towels on hand. Coloured towels are more practical than white, and look good displayed on an open shelf unit.
Above If space permits, it's sociable to include a sofa or armchair in the bathroom.
Opposite A vintage dressing table, or any small table teamed with a mirror, takes up minimal room and adds a relaxed mood.

This is a room for preening too, so a large mirror is essential. One solution is to mirror the whole wall above the basin, or inset one or two mirrored cabinets. A Hollywood-style wall-mounted mirror surrounded by light bulbs is a good choice for girls. Teen boys will appreciate a shaving mirror on a flexible arm. Consider adding a vanity-style basin to create a dressing-table-style zone. Choose a basin with a built-in cupboard below, or buy a bowl-style basin and set it on a broad countertop.

Do provide ample storage for the inevitable sea of bottles, jars and cosmetics. In a small, modern bathroom, a wall-mounted medicine-style cabinet can hold creams and medicines. A steel and glass trolley is a great way to organize bath products. Niche shelves in useful places, such as above the bath or inside the shower, should be planned while building work is in progress, and can be tiled to match the walls. Wicker or rubber baskets, tucked onto a deep shelf or on the floor, are excellent for spare loo rolls and towels.

Kids who shared as children are very likely to go on sharing as teens. For sure, the onset of the teenage years creates the need for a bedroom that offers privacy, a quiet study zone and somewhere to chill with friends, but that doesn't mean close siblings must separate entirely. Many will want to perpetuate a precious sense of connection generated over the years. Older kids at boarding school may be so used to sharing that they will feel lonely in a room on their own. Same-sex sharing is the most likely combination, but a brother and sister who enjoy one another's company can also cohabit successfully. Don't rule out anything until you've thought through the options – and asked your teenage kids!

Plan a flexible format. As kids move into their late teens and have a more independent lifestyle, they may want to reclaim a private zone or, if a brother or sister leaves for college, a younger sibling can inhabit the entire

'Sometimes the interconnecting room can be nice, when my sister and I are getting along, but when we are not it is difficult. But she's at college most of the time.' **HARRY/ 13 YRS**

> '**Even when we were living with four children in a loft, they never really had rooms. They each had an independent unit that could be moved around in the vast space.**' **THOMAS/ FATHER**

space during termtime. Two interconnecting rooms and a bathroom could eventually become a self-contained living space for the boomerang post-college generation (see Self-contained Spaces, pages 122–137). Having a flexible space also gives you the option to separate the zones if it's necessary. If same-sex kids are happy to share a bedroom, the other room can be used for study and relaxing.

Teenagers are just as territorial as small children. If they are sharing interconnecting rooms or one big space, it doesn't mean the decoration and furniture has to be exactly the same throughout. Encourage your kids to create an individual look. Ensure that each teen gets their fair share of the room's positive (and not so good) features. Factors such as proximity to the window(s), door, or en suite bathroom need to be balanced fairly against how much floor space each one gets. If they can't agree about fundamentals at the planning stages, ask yourself before proceeding whether they should really be sharing a space at all!

Below and right If the kids' rooms all lead off one long corridor, use decorative detailing to define them. Here, each bedroom door has been painted in a different colour, together with a panel of colour on the floor and the wall opposite. Furniture can also be colour-coded for further definition.

Opposite right and far right Put a spin on a boarding-school theme and make communal living funky. The same locker-style cupboards and simple chairs appear in each room, yet the colours create very individual moods. A long corridor can be enlivened by clever lighting or by mirroring one wall.

If space permits, separate teen bedrooms from the parental zone so that all their rooms and bathroom(s) are on a separate floor or off one corridor. In an open-plan apartment, zone accommodation so that the living area and kitchen are at the heart of the home, with parents' quarters to one side and teenagers' to the other.

At its most basic, the concept of a shared space is to have two bedrooms that interconnect. This gives kids the best of both worlds: they can communicate easily, but shut the door when they want privacy. If your teens like the idea, it isn't a big job to create a new opening between two rooms. There are choices to be made. A sand-blasted glass door protects privacy and lets in light (you can decorate an ordinary toughened glass door with stick-on vinyl window film). Or get a carpenter to make an MDF door with decorative grooves. If there's enough wall space, consider double doors that fold back flat against the wall. If there's no room for a door, porthole-style round windows provide a visual link.

Older kids love the idea of having their own 'suite' of rooms, so an en suite bathroom to share is a brilliant addition. The best option is a shower room tucked between

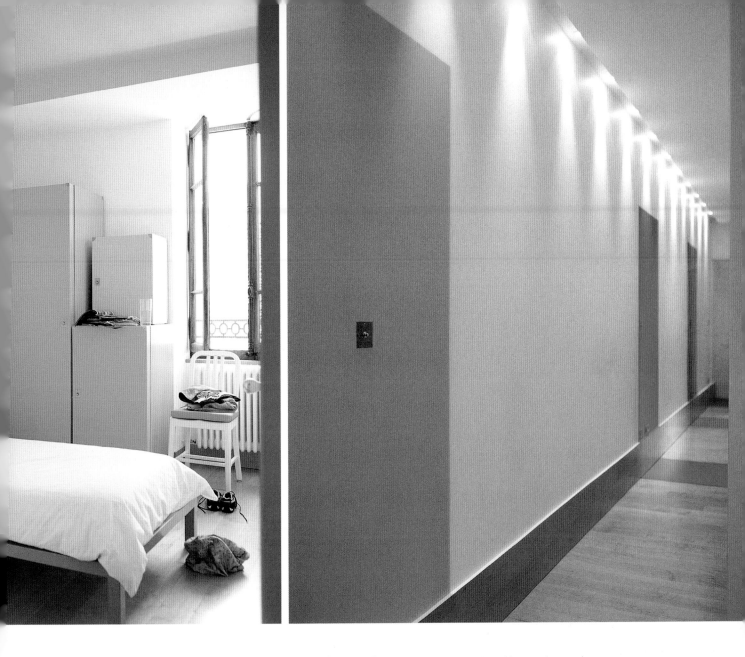

both bedrooms, preferably with access from each room. In a conventional house, it may be necessary to amalgamate two adjoining bedrooms, 'steal' the central portion to turn it into a bathroom, and refigure the sleeping zones. In a loft apartment where the space is more malleable, you might design twin rooms side by side, with a bathroom opposite and a common lobby. A bathroom squeezed between two rooms will lack natural light: think about using glass bricks or sand-blasted glass panels to increase light flow.

Decoratively speaking, interconnecting rooms should reflect each owner's personality. But it's also a good idea to promote a strong visual link that will connect the two rooms when the door(s) stand open. Perhaps the simplest device is to repeat the architectural detailing throughout. Make radiators, light switches, door handles and lighting fixtures match.

Left In an open-plan loft, it's harder to maintain areas of peace and privacy, both of which are essential for teenagers and parents. At the same time, a high ceiling and lack of internal walls makes it easier to design a 'pod' arrangement such as this one. This family has created a series of individual bedrooms for older kids. Each pod has a platform bed accessed by a ladder, with a bed-level window. The double doors mean that each child can be private, but when the doors are open there's a sociable space to share.

Above If there is a series of identikit rooms, it's important for each teen to personalize their interior with favourite furniture or special wallpaper.

HOT TOPICS/ ZONING YOUR SPACE

If you're sharing, it's important to set well-defined boundaries. If you want two of everything (wardrobe, chest of drawers, somewhere to sit), then the division is obvious: there will be your half of the room, and the other person's half. A more fluid arrangement is to have a shared entertaining space, perhaps with a TV and beanbags, a shared wardrobe and a long bench-style desk where you both study. Only the immediate area around your own beds is the individual zone. What suits you best? Make a list of room rules, so if one person needs to study the other doesn't have friends over that night. If boundaries are agreed at the start, you're less likely to argue.

Above left and right There's an art to creating a cosy sleeping pod. Make sure there's enough height between the bed and the ceiling to allow for making the bed, and to prevent the occupant from feeling claustrophobic, especially if they have reached adult height! If possible, plan the space so there's a window or skylight to let in natural light. Don't forget ventilation, as a platform bed is potentially stuffy in summer. A shelf to hold books, a drink and a clock, plus a wall-mounted light, is also essential.

Opposite left and right The beauty of a platform bed is that the space beneath can be devoted to a desk and a seating area with beanbags and floor cushions. These little pods provide plenty of space for friends or siblings to congregate.

In addition, you could commission a carpenter to build matching cupboards and shelves in both rooms. What matters most is that the same motif is identifiable in both rooms. Choosing flooring that is continuous throughout also creates a pulled-together look.

If your teenagers have similar tastes, it can be fun to plan twin rooms along a common theme. Many wallpaper companies do funky geometric designs suitable for teens. Go through the designs with your kids: is there one pattern in two different colours that will work well together? Choose black on white for one room, white on black for the other, or paper alternate walls in hot pink spots on orange, with orange and pink painted walls in between. Large-scale digital-print wallpapers, featuring a cityscape or sea scene, are fun and striking. Metallic paint, panels of textured wallpaper or banners of fabric, from hand-painted artists' canvases to a psychedelic-print dress fabric, are other creative solutions to repeat.

For a more individual look, it's a better idea to pick a decorative style – anything from hippie chic to urban street style – and suggest the kids themselves interpret the bedrooms

along those lines. Encourage them to do a joint mood board first, using fashion, pop or sport images, or, even better, get them to have a magazine-style brainstorming session to come up with a theme. Crystallizing a look into a phrase, such as Powder Room, Rock Chic or Skateboard Dude, is the fastest way to understand the visual impact they want to achieve. Provided furniture and accessories are chosen to follow the theme, each room can use different colours. Dark red for a teen boy and purple for a girl can look amazing played out with a mural of rock posters, coloured light garlands, and an armchair upholstered in faux-leopard print and black velvet.

If there is just one large room suitable for teens to share, then clever ways to divide the space will be of prime importance. The most obvious solution is to install floor-to-ceiling sliding or double doors to bisect the space. Another option is to install a laminated glass 'wall' encased in a metal frame, with a central glass door. Curtains or blinds on both sides can be drawn for privacy, and are a good way to introduce colour or texture. If noise control is important, then solid timber doors or laminated acoustic glass with a noise-reducing membrane are the best choice. If noise isn't an issue, then modern blind companies are a good source for Japanese-style sliding screens in stiffened fabrics.

Think through the practicalities. If there is only one door and only one window, partitions need to be devised so that each teenager can get in and out of the bedroom without too much disturbance, and natural light should be equally distributed between each half. One solution is to design MDF sliding panels with 'windows' higher up, so that light can travel through. Another in a top floor room – is to add a skylight to the windowless section of room. Plan a flexible lighting scheme. Ensure that overhead lights can be dimmed, or install ceiling lights in each half on separate circuits. A reading lamp and bedside light is also essential.

Right and below A shared desk area and built-in bookshelves make the most of a small space. Yet it's important for each sibling to have personal storage space, too; here each bed has a pull-out drawer, and there are more display- and bookshelves above each bed.

Opposite above In a shared room where one occupant is mostly away at college, plan a bedroom that can be fully used by the other sibling. In this boys' bedroom, the absent sibling's bed is used as a daybed, but is reclaimed when he comes home.

Opposite below Sliding doors provide flexibility. By day, they 'disappear' into a pocket in the wall; while at night, they are pulled across to leave a doorway to an en suite bathroom.

WHY DON'T YOU...
>> Have a joint de-clutter session before moving into a newly designed space, so that there is plenty of room to grow into.
>> Respect shared areas, such as a joint desk or shower room, and tidy up.
>> Save space by allocating one cupboard for pooled resources, such as stationery, disks and printer cartridges.

When same-sex teens get on well, a more creative solution is to create individual 'pods' within a room so there is no need for a physical partition. These can take several forms. One solution is to create a built-in bed with shelves, cupboards and a desk at each end of the room. Use a curtain or blinds to screen the pod from the rest of the room. The centre of the room can be devoted to a sofa and beanbags. More radically, get a carpenter to build bed 'pods' on giant castors, so teens can choose where they will sleep at night.

Far left and left The relaxed, individual decoration in each room is proof that teenagers sharing can still have a personalized space without compromise. However, an arrangement like this only works if siblings get on well and can agree on the number of friends coming over, amount of noise and so on.

Opposite Glass doors and panelling make a subtle yet successful room divider between a teenage boy's room and his older sister's bedroom. Sheer curtains provide privacy, while allowing plenty of light to flow through both rooms. For a more modern look, panels of sand-blasted glass are ideal. Sheets of stick-on vinyl film look good on plain glass.

WHY DON'T YOU...

>> Draw up a floor plan of the interconnecting spaces, then swap plans. Design your sibling's room for them, complete with storage, colour and pattern ideas.

>> Award plus points to good features, like a big window, and minus points to bad ones, like proximity to a door. The total final scores must be equal!

Above It's important for each sibling to have their own display space, for cards, photos and memorabilia.

Right In this shared teenage girls' room, interconnecting rooms are accessed to the left and right of a central doorway. Tucked between the two bedrooms is a shared en suite bathroom.

Opposite above and below Although each girl has her own desk and bed, the teenagers share a wall of built-in mirrored cupboards. A floor-to-ceiling mirrored door can be left open for sociability or closed when privacy is required.

COOL ISN'T
ON THE MAP.
YOU CAN'T ASK
DIRECTIONS.

‘ **The mirrored door is handy when the girls want privacy, but they can interact when friends come over.** ’ DEBBIE/ MOTHER

In a loft-style apartment where there are high ceilings, there may be the opportunity to construct a new mezzanine level. This can be a brilliant place to accommodate a teenage sleeping platform or even just a chill-out space away from the parents. If the mezzanine is immediately above a family living area, you will need to screen it from noise and views from below. A glass wall around the perimeter can offer some noise reduction and improves light flow, so is good for a den-style room. Surround a sleeping platform with timber panels that provide privacy and ensure darkness at night. Design cut-out sections to let in natural light during the day and to improve ventilation.

' We built the sleeping platforms as an alternative to separate rooms, for the sake of a homework room. As a teenager, I always felt cut off from everyone studying alone in my room. I would rather my children keep each other company while working in a common area. '

ELIZABETH/ MOTHER

This page and opposite In an apartment converted from an old school, the high ceilings have been put to good use. A new mezzanine level supports divided sleeping platforms for three siblings, while below there is an open-plan area for homework, portholes for communication (opposite), and quiet places to sit and chill. Kids will appreciate an all-white scheme if there are funky details too. Space to prop up art, a mirror ball and inspired lighting create a relaxed, trendy den.

Above If it's possible to plan a new structure for a shared work/sleep space, do so with a sense of fun. This zone has a fireman's pole leading from the sleeping area to the homework zone.

Above right A shared study space is a good idea – it's more sociable working together. Separating the work area from the sleeping zone makes life more relaxing for busy teens.

In an ideal world, allowing teenagers to have the run of an entire floor, or a portion of a single-level apartment, is an ideal option. You are less likely to be bothered by noise and comings and goings at antisocial hours. And, more importantly, it gives teenagers the chance to personalize the entire space rather than just their rooms. Any communal area – a corridor with rooms leading off it, or even a tiny landing – can be decorated as they please, leaving the remaining common parts of the house tasteful and sophisticated!

If the kids' level is reached by a staircase, it's fun to mark the change of decorative tone on that flight of stairs. In place of carpet, stair treads might be painted in black or scarlet, or lined with zinc. Agree with your teens that the walls on the stairs can be decorated with images of their choice, but arranged attractively. It can be a brilliant place to show off avant-garde school artwork or family photographs. If access to the teen zone is on the same level as the rest of the apartment, sliding doors or a full-height door could mark the boundary. Make the door a focal point. Coat it with blackboard paint so you can scrawl reminder messages to your kids, or (in a modern apartment) face it with stainless steel to give a hint of urban cool.

The advantage of a teen-only floor is that, in addition to the kids' bedrooms and bathroom, there will be available space for extra storage. Utilize every spare centimetre: a corridor could be lined with floor-to-ceiling bookshelves and a landing fitted with locker-style cupboards for outdoor kit. A landing, however small, can be transformed into an extra sitting zone. Supply big floor cushions or a mattress with a groovy patterned cotton cover, some atmospheric lighting, such as light garlands or a colour-change LED light, and a small coffee table. If bedrooms are tiny, this is one way for all your kids to get together if they want a parent-free zone.

Above and below right
Same-sex siblings who get on well will enjoy a shared sleeping platform on a mezzanine floor, divided off by low partition walls. Pay particular attention to lighting. If there are ceiling lights designed to illuminate the floor below, put them on a dimmer switch; then, if one person wants to go to sleep earlier, the lights can be dimmed accordingly.

During the teenage years, it's highly likely there will be a shift in the way communal spaces are used at home. When once a large kitchen/living room was sufficient – so you could cook and simultaneously supervise the children – now your kids may want a separate space to chill in with their friends. Or, indeed, with you! The benefit of encouraging kids and their mates to gather in a den, rather just their bedroom, is that it creates a more sociable vibe at home. If teenagers know you operate an 'open house' policy (within limits!), they are more likely to hang out at home rather than in more unsuitable places. Plus, it's fun to spend time watching TV or playing pool with your kids. These are the sociable years before they leave home, so enjoy them while you can!

Do you want a games den or a media zone? There are other variations on the theme depending on family interests: maybe a band practice area, a music room or a yoga space?

'As a parent, it has become clearer and clearer to me that, wherever the TV is, THAT is the heart of the family!'

SERA/ MOTHER

'The family room is our own private room
where we can all play games,
watch TV, read, or just hang out.'

ISABEL/ MOTHER

Get the kids together and discuss all your needs. The benefits of a dedicated media room are that – if you have teen boys addicted to PlayStation – the sitting-room TV won't be permanently monopolized. Likewise, girls who want a night in with a DVD may prefer to hunker down with a bowl of popcorn in a cosy TV room. Best of all, the whole family will have somewhere comfortable for watching TV.

A games den is a more dynamic space, and

needs to be bigger. For parents already fighting the couch-potato gene in their kids, it's a particularly attractive option. It can be as versatile a space as you choose. The central focus will be a games table, but if there's room for sofas, a piano, computer and so on, it can also become a relaxing space to chill out in. The key to devising a room where kids actively want to congregate lies in creating a warm, ambient environment filled with fun, groovy furniture and colour. Don't be tempted to kit it out with your cast-off furniture. Instead, make a conscious effort to design a space that everyone loves.

Left When a media room is not in use, a large blank screen or wall of built-in cupboards can look stark. Balance that effect with upholstery fabrics in bright patterns and a large, groovy wall hanging.

Below left When a TV is positioned close to the floor, either fill the wall above with built-in cupboards or line it with open shelves. A media room full of books, as well as films, will up the cultural ante: you never know, the kids might even read them!

Opposite Don't spend a fortune decorating a media den: a bold wall design, such as this horizontal stripe, will create plenty of impact.

Choose funky decor. Filled with high-tech equipment, a media zone should be decked out in zany colours and modern furniture. If your taste is usually sleek and sophisticated, break out of your comfort zone and decorate this room in complete contrast, even with a dash of kitsch.

Where you locate a games room or media zone is just as important as how you kit it out, or the size of the room. It should be a sociable space where kids can make some noise, so try to keep it well away from quiet zones like the bedrooms or a home office. The vogue for basement conversions continues unabated, and specialist basement companies confirm that families find it useful to house a media room in the bowels of the home. Having a games room upstairs in a converted loft is an equally popular choice (see Lofts and Basements, pages 106–121). But there are plenty of other options, so it's worth considering the entire layout of the house before making a decision.

If you're moving to a new home, it's tempting to devote the majority of living space to a large sociable kitchen, then turn a second living room into a 'smart' sitting room. In the average house, that leaves no space for a den.

But how often are you going to use that smart sitting room? Life is hectic these days, and many working families find they cook and eat late, check emails and watch TV in the kitchen, only using the sitting room to entertain. Provided there is room to include a sofa in your kitchen, plus a TV, and you are relaxed sitting in there, then it makes sense to devote your second sitting area to a den.

For those reworking space in an existing home, this can be the moment to convert a newly redundant playroom, an infrequently used dining room or even an integral garage. If a spare bedroom is the only option, even a small boxroom has the potential to be converted into a media room. Remember, important features such as big windows and plenty of natural light won't matter. A media den is likely to be deliberately darkened, or used mostly at night. If there is room in the garden for a new structure (many summer-houses or home office buildings can be heated and electrically wired), the freedom of a separate room outdoors will be particularly valued by independent teens.

Choose the technology for the media room first, as the TV will be the focal point. How much do you have to spend? If there's the budget for a plasma or LCD television, surround-sound speakers and – the Rolls-Royce of media rooms – an integrated media system, then everyone reaps the benefit. Get a specialist home entertainment company to install the complex technology for you. If you're on a restricted budget, the main investment should be a wall-mounted widescreen TV, which frees up floor space and looks really cool. Alternatively, a conventional TV should be mounted on a low stand on castors (the high street has plenty of good-looking choices) for viewing flexibility.

The ideal height for a wall-mounted TV is relatively low, so that it is at eye level for viewers sitting or lying on a sofa. It makes sense to surround the screen with a wall of built-in

HOT TOPICS/ PARTIES

It's fun to have friends over. However, yours and your parents' definition of a gathering may be very different. Be completely upfront about roughly how many people are coming, where you'll hang out, what you're planning to eat and/or drink, and what time the whole thing will end. It's your responsibility as much as your parents' to hide alcohol not intended for the party, put away precious things, push back the furniture, and clear up afterwards. Get inventive with simple decorations. Bunting looks fun and is inexpensive, add cheap tea lights for atmosphere and cover the food table with a decorator's dustsheet or a runner of bright sari silk.

Opposite above left In an open-plan loft, a media nook has been created with built-in cupboards and furniture grouped around a screen. Bold art on the walls and sleek furniture make this a cool area for teens and adults alike. Dark upholstery is smart but practical.

Opposite below left In a television room, the TV has become a modern-day focal point, so a fireplace may not be appropriate. But if you've gone the low-tech route, and only have a small TV, an open fire can promote a cosy, welcoming ambience.

Right In a teen-only den, dispense with formal seating and invest in faux fur, leather, PVC or giant fabric beanbags.

❛ It's essential to have somewhere to go and watch a film or TV in peace and quiet, especially if you have an open-plan kitchen. ❜ **HELEN/ MOTHER**

WHY DON'T YOU...

>> Check out party websites for fun extras for the TV room. A popcorn maker or bubblegum machine costs less than a pair of trainers. Or fill a bowl with lollipops.

>> Persuade your parents to buy a universal remote for the TV, DVD, and so on, so no one can lose one of the controls.

>> Research funky but inexpensive mood lighting. The best versions combine LEDs and/or a mini laser to provide colour-change or strobe effects: brilliant for creating atmosphere when the film is over.

cupboards: these can hide essential technology, from the DVD player to a stereo system, as well as DVDs, CDs and games consoles. In a dedicated media room, there's little point concealing the TV behind a panel; widescreen televisions look really smart. Cupboard fronts can vary from sleek wood veneer to spray-painted or fabric-covered MDF. Darker shades look particularly effective: experiment with navy, maroon, graphite or forest green.

Choose furniture that offers comfortable viewing positions. If the TV is wall-mounted, one long, deep sofa placed opposite is the best choice. Pick a design with low, upholstered arms, good for lounging on, and team it with beanbags or floor cushions, so extra viewers can loll on the floor. If the TV is mounted on a stand or castors, or can be angled, then an L-shaped seating arrangement works well: modular seating is ideal, or combine two small sofas.

Opposite Nowadays there is less need for a designated computer room at home. Laptops provide more freedom for teens.
Above Kids should go along when choosing furniture; they will soon track down the most comfortable pieces for stretching out on. Modular units are an excellent choice.

'For me, being the mother of teenagers finally forced me to grow up! Its like sharing a flat all over again, with a bunch of untidy students.'

SERA/ MOTHER

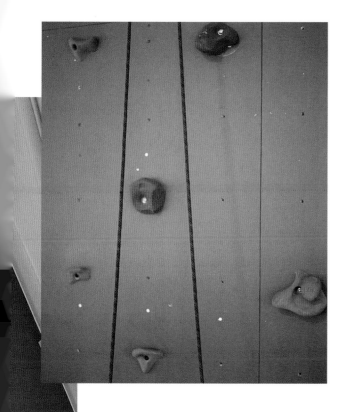

Left and opposite In this new-build modern house, home to four teenage children, a double-height area has been devoted to a climbing wall. Discuss requirements with a specialist climbing-wall supplier, who can advise on the correct equipment. If space permits, as here, it's a fabulous idea to create a vast games area, where every family member can pursue a different activity. That way, kids are less likely to hole up in their bedrooms.

Below Add a quiet zone for chatting and listening to music. Teens will appreciate groovy seating, such as these retro-style cane chairs.

Add low side tables for drinks and takeaway snacks. Keep other furniture to a minimum: built-in shelves for books are a useful addition, but otherwise try to keep this room dedicated to media viewing alone.

Plan lighting carefully. Blinds or thick curtains with a blackout lining are the most sensible choice for successful daytime viewing, or go for Venetian blinds or shutters. Choose light fittings that will create an atmospheric effect, rather than bright overhead lighting. Modern wall lights can be combined with trendier options such as a trail of garland lights around the perimeter of the room, colour-change LED lamps for post-film atmosphere or a light-up neon sign.

A TV den should be the ultimate chill-out zone, so pick cosy, welcoming fabrics. Dense textures, rather than hard, shiny surfaces, are helpful, as they absorb sound. Robust, tactile upholstery fabrics include chenille, velvet, cord or damask; either treat with a stain-guard treatment or choose a dark colour that won't be ruined if someone spills a drink! This could be the one room where you invest in carpet, as it's cosy to lie on (teenagers will love a 1970s-style shagpile),

or cover a wooden floor with a patterned wool rug. Have a few lambswool or chenille throws, but remember those teenage boys and save the cashmere blanket for your own bedroom! Fabric-lined walls can be an excellent idea, increasing the womb-like feeling. Hessian, wool and felt come in a good range of deep colours, or go funky with suede.

The focus in a games room is inevitably the game table itself, so a reasonably large room is essential. Teens will really appreciate a pool or table-tennis table, perhaps combined with table football. Research the sizes of game tables on the internet. Table-tennis tables come in a variety of sizes (some in extra-narrow widths), and most fold away. Pool tables vary in size from 1.2 to 2.7 metres long. What matters most is that there is enough space for players to draw back and set up a shot, so as a rule of thumb the room should be 3 metres wider and longer than

‘ The pool house reminds us of vacation at the beach. It's great for anything from ping pong to parties. Our friends like the multi-purpose quality of the space. ’

TUCKER, BO AND GIBSON/ 17, 15 AND 13 YRS

DRUCKER'S GENERAL STORE

This page A sofa or a couple of squishy armchairs are an excellent addition to a games room. Try not to make it the dumping ground for things you no longer want to give house room to!

your table. If space is tight, buy a slightly shorter cue. Pool tables come in wood veneers, colours or aluminium finishes, plus a choice of fabric colours.

Provide storage to keep accessories in order. Pool cues can be wall-mounted on a cue rack or stand, while table-tennis balls, bats, nets and so on can be stashed in baskets and stored on shelves or in a cupboard. Choose whimsical storage for a light-hearted touch: a retro sideboard painted a bright colour, or a trunk that can double as seating. If it's possible to build shelves into a niche in the wall, conceal them with a curtain of kitsch plastic beads. The games room is also the place to store board games, CDs and a sound system, and musical instruments for band practice.

A games room is likely to attract a gang of kids, so make sure there's a sofa or armchairs to chill out on. If there's a table-tennis table, the floor should provide a good grip, so painted floorboards, vinyl or rubber tiles are practical choices. Plan decoration with a light touch, using upbeat colours. Wacky extras, like a reconditioned jukebox (a major investment, but fun) or a retro-style fridge, will also be appreciated by trendy teens.

Above and above right
If budget and space permit, then building a swimming pool is a fantastic treat for teenagers and parents alike. The advantage of an outdoor pool is that it's fun in summer and friends can hang out in the garden. An indoor pool is more likely to provide year-round amusement.

Opposite If the garden is big enough, use the space to create an additional outdoor chill-out zone. Many garden structure companies offer a huge choice of pavilions, summerhouses, sheds and other retreats. But this isn't sole teenage territory, because adults need a bolthole too.

WHY DON'T YOU ...
>> Reclaim the childhood tree house and use it in summer for lazy days with friends. It's often possible to pick up canvas-covered outdoor cushions at a knock-down price in the summer sales.
>> Persuade your parents to invest in a hammock, then hang it at the bottom of the garden.
>> Convert an existing garden shed by painting the walls inside and adding canvas directors' chairs – a great place for summer revision.

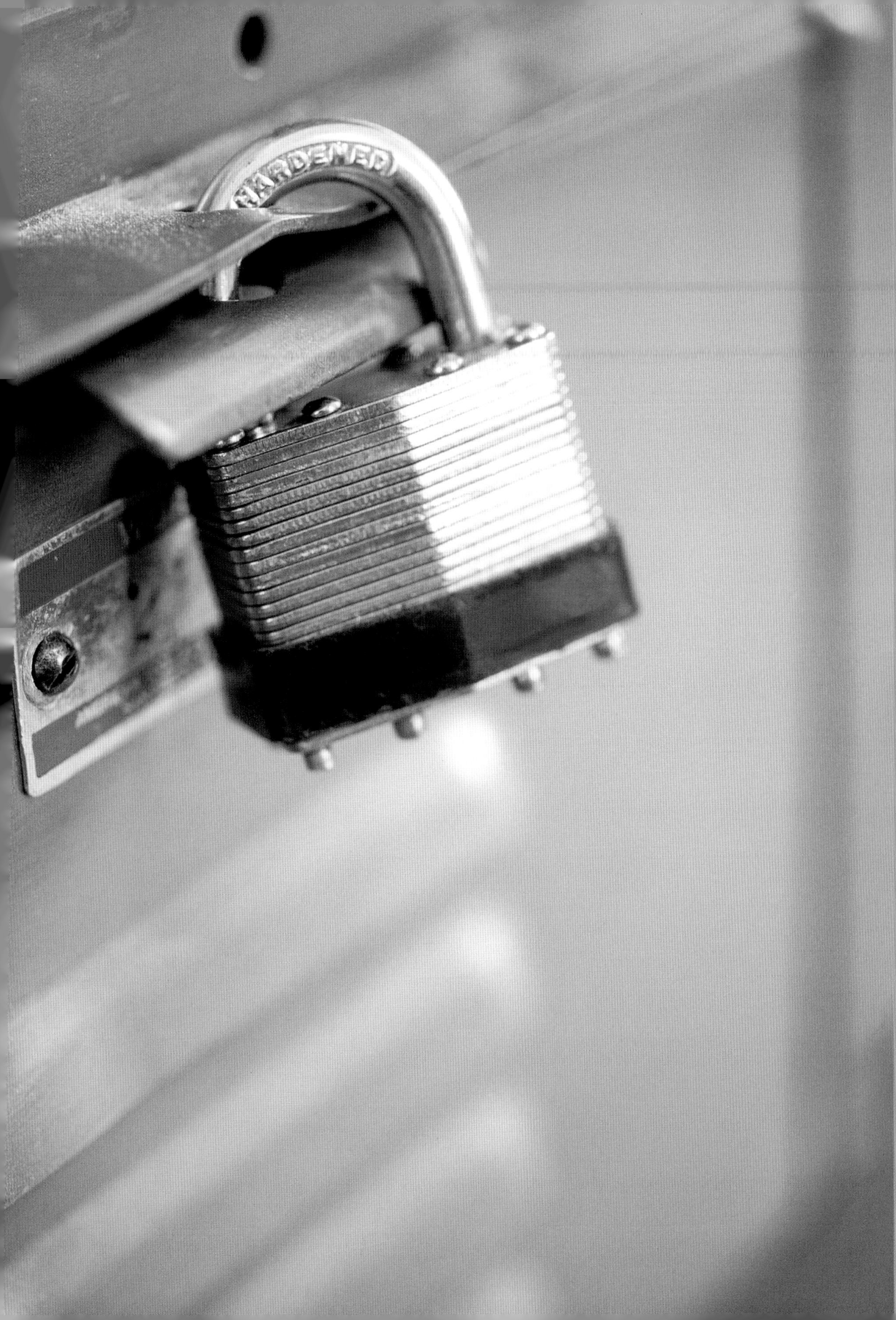

Lofts + Basements

There's an alluring appeal to a loft

or basement space. Tucked right at the top or bottom of a house, it's an area that retains a sense of privacy and separation from the hurly-burly of family life. It's not a traffic area, and other family members won't pass by – it's a destination in itself. A converted loft, in particular, is often the quietest spot in the house. In theory, devoting a secluded zone to your teenagers should please everyone. You won't have to look at their mess or hear their noise, and they will enjoy a sense of independence. For older teens preparing to fly the nest, a basement room that is part of the house, but with a separate entrance, will be a welcome idea.

Yet handing over a loft or basement

space to your teens isn't necessarily the easiest choice. When kids are growing up, taking up more space and in need of increased privacy, it can be a delicate time for re-evaluating priorities. If there's a brand new loft or basement conversion in the

'Our attic is a games room, it's a space for our kids. They use it for watching films of sports training and competitive sports DVDs, and for using the internet.' LUC/ FATHER.

'My bedroom is my haven right at the top of the house ... it's like a little floating room. I don't know if my Dad realizes what a brilliant room he created – it is perfect for a teenager.' **PHOEBE/ 17 YRS**

offing, as parents you may feel you have first call. Perhaps there's a need for a home office, or a new parents' room plus en suite bath in the loft? Only you can decide how much of a sacrifice you're prepared to make. But remember that, within less than a decade, your kids may have left home and then you will have plenty of space in which to spread out!

A loft or basement conversion (or both)

may seem an extravagance, but take time to do the calculations. Balance the costs against the improved quality of life at home and the extra value it will bestow on your property. If you're still not convinced, it's worth asking the opinion of a local estate agent, who will be able to confirm whether adding extra space is an investment in your area. For growing families who might otherwise have to move to get more space, the huge costs of legal fees, tax, removal charges and estate agents' fees will often outweigh the cost of staying put and extending up- or downwards. The earlier you make that decision, the more value you will get from the investment.

Opposite The entire loft in this family home has been devoted to the teenage kids: it's somewhere they can use the computer, have friends to sleep over and watch TV. With timber beams, walls and floor, the decoration is simple. Horizontal beams can be used to suspend hammocks or exercise equipment.

Below left A separate sleeping compartment with a sliding door for privacy, provides a quiet hideaway.
Right Devoting the loft to a games zone means that the less beautiful teenage kit, including computer consoles and DVDs parents would prefer not to watch, can be kept out of adult sight.

Be self-contained. If at all possible, add washroom facilities to a loft or basement so that it is a completely self-contained space: the absolute basics are a toilet and a basin. If ceilings slope sharply, a bath is the best choice. Wall-mount the loo, basin, towel rail and heating; it will make the space feel bigger.

Making the decision to convert a loft or basement space is the easy part. Drawing up plans, obtaining planning permission and project managing the work is more complex. There are two main options. Hiring an architect to plan the look and layout of the new room(s) has many advantages. A professional will evaluate your entire home, provide creative input on the best use for the new space, and come up with enterprising ideas for the look and space-planning, as well as negotiating local regulations and project managing the works. Alternatively, if your budget is tight, most architects are prepared to draw up plans and obtain planning permission, leaving you to do the rest.

Option number two is to call in one of the many specialist loft or basement conversion companies. The advantage here is that such companies generally have broad

specialist knowledge, they may be able to arrange a visit to a similar job so you can visualize the possibilities, and will also project manage the works, bringing in the builders, structural engineer and so on. If you have an immediate neighbour who is considering a similar project, there will be less disruption in the long run if you carry out the works concurrently.

Early on, decide how the loft space will be used: there are advantages and disadvantages to weigh up. It may seem obvious to put your teenage kids up there, with a small bathroom to share, but think through the logistics. If your bedroom is on the floor below, you may suffer noise from above and the comings and goings of friends trailing up- and downstairs. You may prefer to keep the loft space as your own Zen-like eyrie. Another solution is to devote the loft space to a chill-out zone/games room that the entire family can enjoy.

> ' I love the pale plain-painted walls and having my desk up here, and I especially like my big bed. ' **FLORENCE/ 17 YRS**

Left Pitched ceilings and low walls make for an interesting architectural mix. Play that up by emphasizing scale: the giant initial hung above the door makes the ceiling appear taller. If possible, build in cupboards under the eaves, either painted to match walls so they 'disappear', or mirrored to increase light flow and to make the room look bigger.
Below left Don't be put off using big pieces of furniture in a loft space. Here, a double bed feels cosy tucked beneath the pitched roof.
Top right and opposite Awkward corners and restricted wall height can make it tricky to use full-height cupboards. A mix of open shelves, chests and low, locker-style drawers will provide enough storage.

The potential size of the space will also be a deciding factor. If the requirement is for one small, snug bedroom and en suite shower, then a pitched roof and the addition of big Velux windows will be sufficient. For a more substantial project, with the loft divided into several bedrooms and a bathroom, then dormer windows will be necessary. For a funky teen loft space, it's more fun to leave the pitched roof and rafters exposed rather than adding a conventional ceiling, though heat loss will be greater. Do ensure that all windows are big enough to let in sufficient light. As a rough guide, they should be the equivalent in size to 10–20 per cent of the total floor area.

Precisely because a loft space has odd angles, it can be fun to play with the unusual proportions. Rather than trying to squeeze in conventional furniture, try wall-mounted or built-in pieces to fit the space. Consider a high wall-mounted bed tucked below a sloping ceiling, a flip-down desktop, or unexpected cubby-hole wardrobes tucked away beneath the eaves. It seems costly, but the investment of having furniture built in to make the most of every spare centimetre is well worthwhile. Ensure that low alcove cupboards are kitted out with enough shelves that can, in turn, be organized with baskets and boxes. That way, there can be no excuses about messy rooms.

WHY DON'T YOU...
>> Make a feature of a sloping ceiling and paint it in a dark colour for atmosphere. Try inky blue, bronze or even black. Then suspend Chinese lanterns, LED star lights or crystals for night-time drama.
>> Paper the ceiling with giant maps of the world, so you can plan your gap-year route lying in bed. Posters are cheap and decorative: choose a favourite image and buy multiples, then repeat, Warhol-style, all across one wall.

Decoratively speaking, you can be experimental in a loft devoted to teens. Hidden away at the top of the house, this is one space that can look totally different. Let your kids go crazy! Fabric-lined walls will look particularly cool. Provided walls have been clad with a framework of battens, fabric can be tightly staple-gunned around the room, and the finish doesn't have to be perfect. Faux leopardskin or dress satin creates a boudoir effect; camouflage fabric is cool for boys, or use heavy-duty artist's canvas, which can be hand-painted to suit. Choose simple flooring: carpet is best for sound insulation below, or paint the floorboards.

Opposite The pitched roof and exposed beams and pipes commonly found in a loft space can be part of its charm, so aim to emphasize such features rather than cover them up. In this teen girl's bedroom, the stainless-steel heating flue adds a cool design detail. Good heating and ventilation are important in a loft space, which can be chilly in winter and hot in summer. To control light and temperature, choose black-out blinds with aluminium backing for skylights.
Right Custom-built storage is the best way to maximize every square centimetre of space in a loft. Plan for a combination of hanging space, drawers, cubby-holes and open shelves.

WHY DON'T YOU...
>> **Devote one wall to free-standing shelves if there's not enough height for a wardrobe. Industrial shelving companies are brilliant for sturdy, inexpensive steel shelves, lockers and workbenches.**
>> **Collect fruit crates from a local market, paint them, then fix them to the wall in an ordered grid design.**

Once complete, a basement room should feel little different to any other room in the house. The preferred ceiling height should be at least 2.5 metres. Although any basement will need at least one, if not more, light wells to let in natural light, accept that basement rooms will always be darker spaces. So pay attention to lighting: there should be plenty of low-voltage ceiling lights, as well as a mix of task and mood lighting. Good ventilation is crucial. If possible, include French doors to open onto a small light well: however tiny the exterior space, the inclusion of a decorative feature, such as a Buddha, or twinkling exterior lights at night, will enliven an otherwise dead space. An electric ceiling fan inside can be a sensible addition for summer.

Take time to decide on the best use for a basement space. One large basement room may be devoted to a family den/computer room, perhaps combined with a laundry room and an extra shower and WC. This can work well, but do consider the consequences: do you really want

> ‘ I like the privacy of my basement room ... I can play my music really loud without bothering anyone. ’
>
> **TUCKER/ 17 YRS**

Opposite above left In a basement, a teen room will look really cool with exposed brick walls. Play up the mood with industrial-style furniture, funky low-slung seating and dark flooring. A basement room will be darker but not necessarily cooler in summer, so it's important to supply decent fans and ensure the windows open properly. Make the most of a curved niche. This one holds a freestanding cabinet, but a larger niche could even hold a walk-in shower or a basin.

Opposite below left Some basements are divided into a warren of small rooms. This hall, adjacent to the bedroom, creates a compact games area, with an en suite bathroom off to one side.

Below Low-voltage lights, plus a mix of other lamps, are important to supplement natural lighting on dark days.

HOT TOPICS/ TAKING RESPONSIBILITY

Having a loft or basement bedroom brings with it a certain feeling of independence, especially if yours is the only bedroom there. Keeping the area safe, however, becomes your sole responsibility. Have a checklist for when you leave the house: shut the windows (or ask for safety locks so windows can be left ajar), blow out candles and turn off hot electrical appliances like hair straighteners. To save energy, make sure you also turn off TVs, computer consoles and computers at night, rather than leaving them on standby. Eating in your bedroom is OK sometimes, but remove dirty cups and plates regularly, and empty bins; otherwise, your room will become smelly and ultimately a health hazard!

Above A converted basement is a brilliant place to house a media room, as it will be unaffected by lack of natural light and noise is less likely to permeate upwards to the rest of the house. A basement room is also an excellent choice for music practice, or a home gym for the whole family to share.

your teenage kids disappearing into the basement night after night, only to return to the kitchen for sustenance? One alternative is a series of small teenage bedrooms in the basement, with the light, bright rooms upstairs devoted to increased living space. The theory is that bedrooms become sleeping zones, with the rest of your teens' time spent sharing a communal space with you. For sociable, active kids, those who spend time away at college, or teens who shuttle between two family homes, this can be an excellent solution.

The darker nature of a basement room can be used to prompt creative solutions, rather than battling against lack of light. Painting a room white won't magically make it lighter. Using deep, dark colours will promote a cosy ambience. Either play up the basement theme by choosing a modern wall finish, such as polished plaster, or experiment with gloss paint on

walls and floors for a lacquer effect (black and red are good colours). Alternatively, try a large-scale wallpaper: giant damasks or stylized botanical motifs in groovy colour combinations are trendy enough to appeal to teens, too. A mirrored wall in a shady teen bedroom will promote light flow, or try covering the ceiling in mosaic mirror tiles.

Do devote some creative thought to the new staircase leading up to a loft conversion, or down to a basement. For a teen loft bedroom, a securely fixed steel and timber ladder is novel and takes up minimum space. The route to the basement won't necessarily be seen from the hall, so this is another chance to experiment with a wackier style. A cantilevered steel staircase, glass treads, and a handrail illuminated by LED lights or ankle-height low-voltage wall lights flooding light onto the stairs will all provide a dramatic route downstairs.

Above The investment in a basement indoor swimming pool and/or home gym is worth it for sporty, active teens. Make it a fun place for relaxing with the addition of loungers and – the ultimate for everyone – a sauna or steam room. Add ceiling speakers during installation: excellent for pool parties.

Self-contained Spaces

Once teenage kids leave school

a new strand of independence arrives, not just for them but for you too. A sense of separation may come earlier if a teen goes to boarding school or moves regularly between two family bases. Older kids at college will only be at home in the holidays, or you may have other stepchildren to accommodate occasionally. And that's not the whole picture: many older teens or twenty-somethings continue to live at home. In today's economic climate, with high rental rates, even higher property prices and post-college debt, staying put is often the only viable option. That can be tough on both parties. It's not easy to share your house with a bunch of independent young adults.

When that moment of change

comes, make a conscious decision to re-evaluate your space. Life will be much happier if it's possible to allocate an independent living area for your older teen. Minor alterations, such as adding

‘ We wanted a semi-independent "flat" for a growingly independent teenager... it's a place where she can be private, but she still has to have some contact with the parents. ’ GEOFF/ FATHER

'**For us it is great to have our kids upstairs and us downstairs! When their friends are over, they don't keep us up!**' JILLIAN/ MOTHER

a door with a lock to a loft conversion – thus giving it the feel of a 'flat' – will create a sense of independence. Charging a nominal rent or installing a kitchenette are others. Talk to your kids to achieve a workable compromise. Be sensitive to brothers or sisters who may feel jealous of their older siblings' extra independence. Is there a new privilege they can have to soften the blow?

It's worth weighing up the longer-term consequences.
On the one hand, if you make life too comfortable for your kids, will they miss out on one of life's great lessons – earning a living and standing on their own two feet? On the other, your investment may be worthwhile. If you have several kids, each one may pass through the self-contained space as the older ones fly the nest. Eventually, it may evolve into a granny flat or a guest suite. More importantly, in a world where it's harder than ever to maintain a sense of family life, creating an independent zone for your older kids may ensure that you actually see more of them rather than less.

Self-contained Spaces

This page and opposite This compact, brilliantly designed living space is self-contained, screened from an open-plan loft by a sliding door. A shift in floor levels distinguishes the bathroom zone from the living area, while behind the sliding door is the communal kitchen and living space. The tall built-in cupboards carve out a separate space and retain privacy but, because they are not full height, still allow light flow.

Overleaf On one side, the long run of cupboards provides plenty of storage, while on the other they create a corridor, with a full height door at each end, leading towards the WC.

Independent living means a multitude of things to different kids. For some, it's important to have a door to lock and privacy. For others, it means having the freedom and facilities to cook when and where they see fit. Ask your teens to prioritize and help you to create a self-contained space to meet those needs.

The property type will be the determining factor in the self-contained living space you can create. If your house already has a basement or loft conversion, with a conventional bathroom and bedrooms configuration, is it possible to go one step further? By adding minimal kitchen facilities, and turning the bedroom into a sitting zone as well, it will instantly feel more independent. Alternatively, if there is just one very large room – perhaps a redundant playroom – the addition of sliding doors to divide it into different zones makes a big difference. Do you have a built-in garage? Might this be converted into new living quarters?

Remember that for teenagers starting out it is not space and beautiful finishes that matter as much as the possession of a truly independent zone. So do keep both budget and space arrangement under tight control. From a planning

point of view, it's advisable to retain access to the self-contained living space from the main home. If there is a separate entrance, the space will be classed as a self-contained flat and will probably require planning permission. If in doubt, consult the planning department at your local council.

In its most basic form, self-contained living can be achieved, studio-style, in one large room. If there is no separate bathroom, adding a basin provides extra independence. These days, there are so many attractive washstands and vanity unit options that a basin won't look out of place. It can be tucked behind a free-standing screen or even built into a cupboard. Or install a basin in an alcove, concealed behind a beaded curtain. In a cool boy's pad, a utility-

' There are no "walls" separating this area from the rest of the apartment. I'm always surprised when I'm at a friend's place and they "go to their room". '

LUNA/ 13 YRS

WHY DON'T YOU ...
>> Use clever paint
tricks as a brilliant way to
create interest in a plain
room. A broad paint
stripe around the
perimeter of the room
doubles as skirting. Paint
the ceiling in a deeper
hue than the walls, and
then there's no need for
a cornice.
>> To create a
sophisticated, pulled-
together look in a studio
space, choose just three
toning colours, plus one
or two sharp accent
shades, and don't waver
from the palette.

> ❛ **White is good for empty Zen-like spaces, but that's not how this family lives!** ❜
>
> **ETIENNE/ FATHER**

style stainless-steel bowl or ceramic butler's sink are both good options. A girl's boudoir will benefit from a bowl-style basin atop a wood worktop or a washstand with rails beneath for towels.

The inclusion of kitchen facilities, however minimal, marks a huge shift in independence. How self-sufficient does your older teen want to be? If he or she will still be present at main family meals, then go minimal. A kettle, a microwave, a small fridge and a sink are the basics. Plan a specific area for them so that it's easy to keep the food-preparation zone hygienic and clean, and add a good-size bin. Check on the internet for specialist companies that offer small-space living solutions. Clever options include a wall-mounted stainless-steel unit, with integral worktop and tiny sink, plus shelves, which can be combined with a choice of cupboards underneath. Catering companies are a good source of utility-style stainless-steel workbenches that can be combined with a small ceramic sink.

For greater independence, a kitchen zone can also include a dishwasher and more preparation space. Small-space kitchen companies provide ingenious all-in-one units, with everything from a wall-mounted microwave and grill to a hob and a sink, all concealed in a neat cupboard, with metal effect or wood doors. Many kitchen appliances come in slim sizes specifically for small spaces. In a funky, utility-

Opposite Thoughtfully divided up and furnished, it's possible to give just one large room the look of a studio apartment, even if there is no kitchen or bathroom. For a grown-up mood, it's essential to have a separate seating zone away from the bed. Dress up a plain divan with a long bolster and cushions.

Opposite above right To create a lobby mood, add a chair or a narrow console table for bags and keys.

Above left A double bed is essential for college-age kids. Keep the sleeping area simple, relaxed and free from clutter, to emphasize the change in zones.

Right and above right In today's mobile age, a separate land line and vintage telephone may be amusing for teens.

Opposite This older teen girl's room is separated from her parents' loft via double doors – so she can use their kitchen and bathroom – but has a separate entrance. With its hot pink walls and junk-shop furniture choices, the room has been stamped with a young, trendy mood.

Above left A budget junk-store-style sofa looks cool draped with a tie-dye sheet or vintage quilt.

Far left A retro dressing-table pouffe can double up as extra seating, if necessary.

Left and above right A self-contained teen space should reflect the owner's decorative likes and tastes.

Andy Warhol: The Museum of Modern Art, New York

Left Accessed via a long corridor lined with practical wardrobes, this older girl's bedroom and bathroom creates a private retreat away from the rest of the family. Decoratively speaking, the mood is sophisticated, with pale pastel tones and glamorous mirrors.

Opposite left For an older child, perhaps living at home again after college, it's vital to have a quiet study zone as well as a seating area for entertaining friends.

Opposite right Older kids will jump at the chance of a grown-up space with good lighting and chic bedlinen.

chic room – perhaps with loft-style brick walls – teens might prefer a galley-style free-standing workbench with built-in sink, hob and preparation space, or look out for free-standing kitchen units to mix and match. Do provide good ventilation, and fit smoke alarms.

However tiny the space, it's important to provide a comfortable place to sit and eat: no one wants to munch a takeaway on the bed. High-street stores are a great source of foldaway tables and chairs at good prices: buy a few extra chairs for bigger gatherings, too. Garden furniture is another budget option. Chairs can be hung from the walls on sturdy hooks, tucked into a cupboard or pushed under the bed, or choose a stacking style. A slim table, from a trestle table to a glass-topped dining table, can double up as a study space and dining zone. Any piece of multi-functional furniture is an asset; from a trolley on wheels for books or the TV, to a seating cube that unfolds into a spare bed.

It's important to make a distinction between the bed and the relaxing zone. This means providing somewhere else to sit, as well as the bed. A small sofa bed, a daybed, a futon or even a hammock are all excellent choices, as they can accommodate a friend overnight. If possible, the bed should be tucked into a nook or partitioned off. In a girl's zone, attach a suspension wire close to the ceiling, and hang

HOT TOPICS/ BUDGET

It can be a tricky compromise if you've left school – and technically have your independence – but are still living at home. Are you on a student income or earning a salary? Depending on your circumstances, it's seems only fair to come to an agreement with your parents on your living costs. They may not expect you to pay rent, but shouldn't you contribute in part towards household bills, food and so on? If your budget is really tight, then it's always possible to help out in other ways: save on decorator's costs by repainting the walls, cook for the rest of the family occasionally or help out in the garden.

floaty muslin curtains; a teen boy's bed could be partitioned off with floor-to-ceiling sliding panels in artist's canvas. If the space is bigger and needs a more formal division, there are specialist companies who custom-build. Options include folding or bi-folding doors, sliding doors or even folding walls. Many specialist fitted-wardrobe companies also offer good-looking solutions, such as sliding doors in translucent glass, or mirrored options.

Don't spend a fortune on flooring and window treatments. However much you might like your kids to treat this space with respect, it's more realistic to kit out the area as you might a rental flat. Fittings should be robust, so that if accidents happen things can be replaced with as little expense and effort as possible. Lay inexpensive carpet, wooden floorboards or plain

Self-contained Spaces

Below left and right
In a comparatively small industrial-style space, such as a portion of a loft or a converted garage, an open-plan sleeping zone and bathing area works well. It can often be cheaper to custom-make bathroom fittings. Budget basins set into a plain worktop combined with a cabinet on castors will cost a fraction of a designer vanity unit. Look for bargains, such as towel rails or smart hooks, in bathroom showroom sales. Salvaged pieces, such as a reconditioned bath or basin, will also save money.

Opposite Subtle changes in style will take a bedroom all the way from teenage grunge to urban cool. Investing in one fantastic decorative piece – a painting or a vintage bed – will upgrade cheaper accessories.

lino, then your teens can overlay them with a rug if they wish. For windows, stick to roller or Venetian blinds, or supply a wood or metal curtain pole that can be customized with tie-on curtains. Don't forget a vacuum cleaner, so there are no excuses about keeping the place relatively clean.

Once the layout and fittings have been sorted, leave the decoration to your kids. Depending on their circumstances, either supply an agreed budget for them to use, or get them to kit out the space using their own money. Let them do the decorating, the furniture-shifting and the picture-hanging. This not only promotes independence but it makes the whole process more fun. Once your kids are sorted, it will be the greatest of pleasures when they invite you back in!

WHY DON'T YOU …
>> Set yourself a strict budget for decorating and furnishing the entire space, and stick to it. Being frugal will force you to be more inventive. Bargain-hunting on ebay or at car boot sales can be a cheaper way to buy.
>> Get on the mailing list for seasonal designer warehouse sales: a brilliant way to get good-quality furnishings at a fraction of the price.
>> Rummage through your grandparents' attics. Their cast-offs may be hip by now, and junky old pieces can be painted or reupholstered.

If you enjoy the company of your teenage offspring, the secret is to create a welcoming, hard-working family space in which everyone can spend time together. Of course your kids will also want private zones for hanging out with friends. But if you encourage an 'open house' policy, it ensures that they and their friends will feel truly welcome, and they are more likely to congregate in a communal space. It's also crucial that, as a family, you make time to be together. Whether that means having a long kitchen table and booking everyone for a weekly Sunday lunch, or creating a comfy sitting room where you can watch a DVD en masse, what matters is that communication lines stay open and you have down-time together.

These days, a multi-functional kitchen, with an eating and seating zone, has become the most fashionable and practical solution. Kids naturally gravitate towards the kitchen, and usually head straight for the fridge. But if they

'I love the big kitchen, because as the kids get older I feel like I'm with them while they're on the computer, watching TV, having a snack... it really brings a relaxed, sociable quality.' DEB/ MOTHER

'**It has always been an act of coordination to live together, but at least we do live TOGETHER, rather than everybody hidden away in their rooms.**' **THOMAS/ FATHER**

also choose to hang out here, especially with friends, take it as a compliment. This is not the time to create a sophisticated kitchen that will make teens feel out of place. Instead, concentrate on a relaxed, upbeat design with appliances and gadgets that will appeal: a big American-style fridge with ice machine and a wall-mounted widescreen TV are a sure-fire way to ensure the kitchen is always occupied. Make sure there are plenty of seating options to cope.

If your home doesn't allow for a large kitchen, then a family sitting room is the next best thing. The room design, and function, is quite different to a media room, where the television is the star of the show. It's OK to have a TV in a sociable sitting room, but this should be a space where you and your kids can chat, listen to music, read and socialize in comfort. If you're lucky enough to have space for a sitting room and a big kitchen too, then celebrate. However, multi-functional one-space living can be noisy! Make the sitting room a quiet zone, so everyone has a space for escape.

Left A kitchen table should be suitable for eating, doing homework and entertaining. A square table that seats two people on each side is ideal. Combine it with a breakfast bar for flexibility. A standard lamp provides task lighting. **Below left** These inventive kitchen cupboards combine practicality with humour.

Opposite Ideally, the kitchen table should be long enough to accommodate the entire family – plus friends – for a meal. If there's space, provide a separate desk for studying and operate a hot-desking policy: once homework is finished, the desktop should immediately be cleared so it's free for the next person.

Eating together is a fundamental part of family life. Plan the kitchen as the hub of the home, so your kids naturally make a beeline for it. Bold planes of colour, an open-plan layout and simple lines are the easiest way to make it a practical, welcoming space.

The most sociable kitchen design includes generous space for cooking: very important, as it encourages teens to get active in the kitchen. The most modern layout choices are to combine one wall of cupboards with a parallel island unit (which can double as a breakfast bar), or go for a galley-style kitchen running the length of one wall, plus a dining table. The appeal of a streamlined layout is that the remaining floor space can be devoted to a sitting area. Island units are a sociable addition. Ensure that the worktop protrudes by around 25 centimetres so that stools can be tucked beneath, or extend the worktop on a lower level, to create a more substantial dining area teamed with chairs.

Even if you have a breakfast bar, it's a good idea to combine it with a dining table. Teenagers love to perch on

Left and opposite Make it a warm, comfortable place to sit, and everyone will be happy to congregate in the kitchen. Here, there's a choice of bar stools (opposite below) and dining chairs, as well as squishy armchairs (opposite above left) grouped around a television. Metal, wood, plastic or leather-upholstered stools are a practical choice. For armchairs, go for loose covers that are easy to wash. Install an extractor fan, to get rid of late-night takeaway smells.
Opposite above right Teenage life is busy; allocate a desk area or section of worktop for paperwork, timetables, files and phones.

stools for a quick snack, but as adults you will still want to enjoy a dinner party in comfort. One of the joys of teenagers is that there will often be a last-minute assortment of friends for impromptu suppers, so choose a table that can cope. To squeeze in extra guests, a large, round style is a good choice, or an extending rectangular table, preferably a design that can seat up to 12 people. Choose a colourful powder-coated steel frame, or go for a robust toughened glass or stainless-steel-topped table. A chunky, wood refectory-style table, with matching benches, is another excellent option.

Teenagers have always preferred to lounge or loll rather than sit conventionally on a chair. So have fun choosing kitchen seating and take the kids with you to look at options;

HOT TOPICS/ HELPING OUT

You may think of the kitchen as the place to go for food and drink, somewhere to do homework and hang out with friends. For your parents, it's also a working zone: they are responsible for stocking the fridge and keeping the space in order. Get into the habit of helping out. Loading the dishwasher, wiping down surfaces and emptying rubbish takes minutes and will earn you multiple brownie points, especially if you do so without being asked. The kitchen is a communal zone, so it's polite to think twice before emerging in your dressing gown at midday, or entertaining hordes of friends until midnight. Negotiate house rules with your parents, then stick to them.

tall gangly boys in particular need to try them out. Bar stools are popular: choose a row of matching stools for a chic look, or an identical style with each seat covered in a different colour, which is more fun. American diner-style stools are also cool, as are stools on castors. Fold-up bar stools can be tucked in a cupboard for when extra seating is required. If you have a separate dining table too, try to pick a smart chair that appeals to you and the kids. Colourful acrylic or modern-day copies of twentieth-century classic plywood designs are stylish options.

If there is space in the kitchen for a separate seating area, plan the layout to match the activities that will go on here. If you've included a TV in the room, can it be viewed from this zone, as well as the cooking area? A large wall-mounted widescreen TV will provide flexible viewing options. If there's room for a small sofa, provide a coffee table or upholstered footstool as well; the more satellite groups of seating you can provide, the more flexible the room becomes. Choose relaxed, low-slung seating: a daybed, upholstered seating cubes or vintage leather club armchairs are all relaxed choices. Add castors to as much furniture as possible, so everything is easily cleared away for parties.

Decoratively speaking, in a kitchen space you should tread a fine line between function and comfort, so don't go overboard with clinical, hard finishes. Of course, the floor and work surfaces must be hard-wearing. Wood, stone, rubber or concrete are all practical for floors (add a soft rug in the sitting zone). Corian, wood, stainless steel, stone or laminate are the best choices for worktops. Use decorative details to warm up the room. Laying a rubber floor or painting one wall in a vibrant colour, such as orange or cobalt blue, will add depth. A decorative splashback is another way to introduce texture: think of tiny brick-style tiles in lime green, or bronze mosaics. Or create a decorative focus on one of the walls opposite the kitchen area, either wallpapered in a large-scale geometric print or hung with a piece of art.

In a separate sitting room, it's easier to create a low-key, relaxed mood. If possible, include a fireplace. Many of the new designs look equally good in a very modern space or in

Opposite If there's no room for a separate den, focus on designing a large, multi-functional kitchen and seating zone that teenagers will enjoy. A built-in or wall-mounted widescreen TV is an excellent choice for the whole family, but is particularly useful if the kitchen is the designated chill-out space for the kids.

An island unit, including a breakfast bar, means friends can pull up stools and congregate in larger numbers, whether to do homework or watch a film. **Below** Picture the kitchen as a potential party space too: tuck the units to one side or choose free-standing units on wheels so that the room can easily be cleared.

a more traditional environment. The best styles to try are dramatic slit-style flat wall surrounds, plain stone fireplaces jazzed up with a funky circular or oval modern fire bowl or a simple wood-burning stove. For seating, pick low-slung furniture that can be arranged in companionable groups. A collection of modular seating, including corner units and foot stools, is perfect in a contemporary room, or combine a pair of smaller sofas with an armchair. Choose cosy, soft upholstery. Velvet, wool, chenille or faux suede all feel fantastic, and are even more inviting combined with plenty of feather cushions, bolsters and a throw or two.

Creating ambient lighting is vital. In a kitchen and sitting zone, there should be excellent overhead lighting above the cooking area in the form of low-voltage ceiling lights and/or

Above The bonus of a relaxed kitchen is that kids will feel it is as much their territory as their parents'. A long worktop means meal preparation can take place at one end, while a group of kids can be hanging out or studying at the other. In a large open-plan space, the island unit becomes a useful space divider. This one has shelves one side for cookery books, and kitchen storage on the other.

Right Keep the look design-conscious and colourful to appeal to teens and grown-ups. Modern classic furniture has universal appeal.

Opposite Sitting room furniture should allow teens to gather companionably together. Low-slung modular combinations are good choices, plus floor cushions or a daybed. A soft, funky rug – shagpile or sheepskin – is ideal for those who like to sprawl on the floor.

powerful pendant lights. Over the dining table and breakfast bar, more intimate, decorative lighting is needed. This is an excellent place to include a trendy light fitting that will appeal to both you and your teens – a twinkly modern chandelier, organic-shaped ceramic or paper pendant shades or groovy coloured glass lampshades all look smart. Do fit a dimmer switch, so lighting can be adjusted according to whether you're having a family supper or a teen late-night gathering. In a separate sitting room, or to distinguish the sitting zone in a kitchen, keep things mellow. Mix and match styles, perhaps an angled task light for reading, several drum-shaded lamps to cast pools of light and a colour-changing mood light.

Focus on putting together a sociable family room that doesn't look too perfect. It's impossible to keep a heavily used space tidy, and everyone will feel more relaxed if the look is lived in. In a kitchen, that might mean open shelves piled with china and glass, and a pinboard studded with daily schedules. In a sitting room, it might mean a coffee table piled with magazines and a cosy throw on the sofa. The sociable space should be a place where everyone is happy to gather. Keep things welcoming, and they will.

Above In an open-plan sitting room/kitchen, pick flexible seating so kids can congregate away from the main seating area. Modern furniture showrooms are an inspiring source of colourful chairs and pouffes – a more sophisticated alternative to beanbags and floor cushions.
Right A fireplace is always a sociable focus, and a central wood-burning stove is an excellent way to divide up a big kitchen.

WHY DON'T YOU...
>> **Offer to make a family supper (including clearing up!). Master a few dishes that you can do spectacularly well, like a great curry or stir-fry.**
>> **Set the table your way. Sprinkle glitter on the tabletop, scrawl place names onto stones from the beach, or lay a freshly made daisychain around each place setting.**

'A large space like this works so well, because you can have fifteen kids here and barely notice them as you might in a compartmentalized series of rooms. It's also great for parties!' —HELEN/ MOTHER

Above Having teenage kids provides an opportunity for everyone to be experimental and trendy. A colourful environment is fun, so go with the flow, decoratively speaking. Vibrant upholstery can be fun to try: a combination of several different jewel shades, one for each armchair, is an exciting, imaginative choice.

Right Organize furniture in sociable groups, with low-slung sofas and coffee tables. Scatter atmospheric extras, from incense burners to tea lights, throughout so it's easy to dim the lights and relax.

Opposite In a larger room, try curtaining off a smaller space or an alcove, so two conversational groups can happily co-exist.

WHY DON'T YOU...

>> Have a music sampling evening to find sounds that the whole family will enjoy. Less contentious choices might include wave sound effects, yoga or chill-out tracks and tribal or world music.

>> Experiment with ambience-inducing scents. Scented candles come in fragrances from vanilla to green tea; they don't have to be old-fashioned florals. Or burn your own incense for everyone else to try.

>> Relax by candlelight. Tea lights can be bought cheaply in bulk, as can pretty tea-light holders.

153

Sources

WALL FINISHES

British Arts
Dons Yard
Mapledurham
Oxon RG4 7TS
0118 972 45402
www.britisharts.co.uk
Print your own art or photos onto canvas, paper, MDF, Perspex and aluminium.

Graham & Brown
Call 0800 328 8452 or visit www.grahambrown.com for your nearest stockist.
Digital photography murals, geometric wallpapers and metallic effect wall finishes.

House Couturier
285 New Kings Road
London SW6 4RD
020 7371 9255
www.housecouturier.com
Funky giant-scale wallpapers in broad stripes, jewel motifs, cityscapes and trailing leaves.

Maps International
Call 0800 038 6277 or visit www.mapsinternational.co.uk
World, city and satellite wall maps, plus globes.

The Stencil Library
Call 01661 844844 or visit www.stencil-library.co.uk
Mail-order stencil supplier. Their fabulous Bad Attitude designs include camouflage, barbed wire and fingerprint motifs. Also paints, brushes and gilding accessories.

Timorous Beasties
384 Great Western Road
Glasgow G4 9HT
0141 337 2622
www.timorousbeasties.co.uk
Inventive wallpaper and fabric designs. Cushions and lighting, too.

FABRICS/BLINDS

Cheap Fabrics
www.cheapfabrics.co.uk
Online store with every type of fabric and great trimmings.

Ella Doran Design
46 Cheshire Street
London E2 6EH
020 7613 0782
www.elladoran.co.uk
Bespoke digital print blinds plus groovy accessories.

Marimekko
16–17 St Christopher's Place
London W1U 1NZ
020 7486 6454
www.marimekko.co.uk
Scandinavian fabrics in bold, large-scale designs. Also linen, towels and cushions.

Surplus and Adventure
0800 043 0099
www.surplusandadventure.com.
British army camouflage fabric, nets, hammocks and flags

SURFACES/FLOORING

Formica
Call 0191 259 3000 or visit www.formica.co.uk for details of your nearest stockist.
Manufacturer of decorative laminate materials.

The Rubber Flooring Company
0800 849 6386
www.therubberflooringcompany.co.uk
Huge selection of rubber tiles and sheet rubber flooring.

Tarkett Flooring
Visit www.tarkett.co.uk for your nearest stockist.
Vinyl and laminate floors in bright colours, checks, dots, and florals, plus wooden flooring.

Worlds End Tiles
Silverthorne Road
London SW8 3HE
020 7819 2100
www.worldsendtiles.co.uk
Ceramic, colour and glitter mosaics and stone flooring.

FURNITURE

Argos
Call 0870 600 2020 or visit www.argos.co.uk for your nearest store.
Inexpensive beds, beanbags and storage options, plus fun accessories.

Feather and Black
Call 01243 380 600 or visit www.featherandblack.com for your nearest store.
Double and single classic iron and contemporary wood beds, plus mattresses and bedlinen.

Habitat
Call 0845 601 0740 or visit www.habitat.net for your nearest store.
Trendy, fun furniture including occasional seating, desks and beanbags, plus inventive lighting.

Ikea
Call 0845 355 1141 or visit www.ikea.co.uk for your nearest store.
Modern storage, beds, desks, lighting and accessories at modest prices and in funky, colourful designs.

The Lounge About Company
01323 872800
www.lounge-about.com
Cotton and leather beanbags, cowhide rugs and cushions, and faux leather floor cushions

MAIL ORDER

Handmade Hammocks
01557 860000
www.handmadehammocks.co.uk
Rope, fair-trade cotton and string hammocks, plus hammock chairs and cushions.

Next Home
Call 0845 600 7000 or visit www.next.co.uk for your nearest store.
Mid-price home accessories, including cushions, beanbags, faux-fur throws, futons, shower curtains, and bedding.

ACCESSORIES/LIGHTING

Bombay Duck
Call 020 8749 3000 or visit www.bombayduck.co.uk for your nearest stockist.
Gorgeous, girly accessories.

The Glow Company
01302 771446
www.theglowcompany.co.uk
Glowing and colour-change lights, lava lamps, candles, glow sticks and lounge lights.

The London Graphic Centre
Call 020 7759 4500 or visit www.londongraphics.co.uk for your nearest store.
Spray paints for home graffiti, plus art materials, plan chests and excellent desk lamps.

Mathmos
22-24 Old Street
London EC1V 9AP
020 7549 2700 www.mathmos.com
The original lava lamps, plus colour-change lights and space projectors, which project moving patterns on to walls and ceilings.

Oliver Bonas
Call 020 7627 4747 or visit
www.oliverbonas.co.uk for your
nearest store.
*Fashion and home stores with
inexpensive, pretty accessories.*

Purple Puffin
0870 2404553
www.purplepuffin.co.uk
*Bead curtains, wind chimes, incense
burners and candles.*

Urban Outfitters
36-38 High Street Kensington
London W8 4PF
020 7761 1001
www.urbanoutfitters.co.uk
*Fun, colourful accessories such as
cushions, shower curtains, wall hooks
and crockery.*

SMALL SPACE SOLUTIONS

Hafele
01788 542020
www.hafele.co.uk
*Vast array of ironmongery, from
cupboard handles to internal fittings
like wire drawers and hanging racks.*

The Loft Shop
01903 738500
www.loftshop.co.uk
*Roof windows, spiral and traditional
staircases, blinds and other specialist
loft equipment.*

The London Basement Company
020 8847 9449
www.tlbc.co.uk
Basement conversion company.

Saniflo
Call 020 8842 0033 or visit
www.saniflo.co.uk. for your
nearest stockist.
*Specialist sanitaryware for bathrooms
and WCs in awkward spaces like lofts
and cellars.*

Space Savers
020 7624 1002
www.spacesavers.co.uk
*Small-space kitchen solutions,
including ingenious kitchen-in-a-
cupboard options.*

Wallbeds Direct
62–168 Regent Street
London W1B 5TG
020 7434 2006
www.wallbeds-direct.com
*Wall beds in single and double sizes,
including side-folding options and
cupboard surrounds.*

SCREENS

Eclectics
Call 01843 608 789 or visit
www.eclectics.co.uk for your
nearest stockist.
*Roman, roller and Venetian blinds in
funky colours and patterns, plus Kyoto
sliding panels for room dividers.*

Space Slide
01922 743211
www.spaceslide.co.uk
*Made-to-measure sliding wardrobe
doors plus sliding dividers in wood or
clear or sand-blasted glass.*

Spazio
01580 763593
www.spazio.co.uk.
*Room-dividing options include made-
to-measure folding doors, sliding
doors, room dividers and bi-fold doors.*

Trade Blinds Direct
01423 562555
www.tradeblindsdirect.co.uk
*Sliding fabric panels for windows or to
use as room dividers plus digitally
printed blinds.*

BATHROOMS

Aston Matthews
141-147a Essex Road
London N1 2SN
020 7226 7220
www.astonmatthews.co.uk
*Modern and traditional bathroom
fittings plus groovy coloured basins.*

Colourwash Bathrooms
Call 020 8830 2992 or visit
www.colourwash.co.uk for your
nearest store.
Modern fittings with trendy detailing.

Ideal Standard
Call 01482 346461 or visit
www.ideal-standard.co.uk for your
nearest stockist.
Well-designed small-space solutions.

Twyford Bathrooms
Call 01270 879777 or visit
www.twyfordbathrooms.com for
your nearest stockist.
Good mid-priced bathroom suites.

GAMES AND MEDIA EQUIPMENT

Comet
Call 08705 425425 or visit www.
comet.co.uk for your nearest store.
*Widescreen, LCD and plasma TVs,
portable TVs, TV brackets and wall
stands, plus stereo equipment.*

Games Tables 4 U
0870 1188118
www.gamestables4U.com
*Online suppliers of games tables –
football, air hockey, table tennis, pool
and snooker, plus accessories.*

John Lewis
Call 0845 60 49049 or visit
www.johnlewis.com for your
nearest store.
*Good selection of indoor games
including table-tennis, pool, air
hockey and football tables.*

Pool Table Services
425 High Road
Harrow Weald
Middlesex HA3 6EJ
020 8861 0006
www.pooltableservices.co.uk
*Pool, snooker, table tennis and
football tables plus accessories.*

STORAGE

The Holding Company
241–245 Kings Road
London SW3 5EL
020 8445 2888
www.theholdingcompany.co.uk
*Storage specialists. Under-bed bags,
shoe boxes, wardrobe systems, trunks
and baskets.*

Homebase
Call 0845 077 8888 or visit
www.homebase.co.uk for your
nearest store
*Budget storage, including wood boxes
on wheels, plastic stacking crates and
under-bed storage.*

Lakeland Limited
Call 015394 88100 or
www.lakelandlimited.co.uk for your
nearest store.
*Useful storage. Under-bed boxes on
wheels, wicker baskets and shoe racks,
plus extras for small-space kitchens.*

Muji
41 Carnaby Street
London W1V 1PD
020 7323 2208
www.muji.co.uk
*Simple and stylish storage options
in acrylic, cardboard and canvas.*

Rapid Racking
01285 686868
www.rapidracking.com
*Industrial fittings including metal
lockers, chrome trolleys and shelving,
tables and stacking plastic boxes.*

Picture Credits

All photographs by Winfried Heinze.
Key: a=above, b=below, r=right, l=left, c=centre.

1 The O'Connor Bandeen family home in London; 2–3 The home of Ben Johns and Deb Waterman Johns; 4 l Freddie Hair's room in London; 4 bc Isabel & Ricardo Ernst's family home; 4 r The home of Ben Johns and Deb Waterman Johns; 5 al Glasserman/Gilsanz Residence; 5 ar Isabel & Ricardo Ernst's family home; 5 cl & br The Eclair-Powell home in London; 5 c The designer Etienne Mery's home in Paris; 5 r Stella's room in NYC; 6 l & 7l The Marsden family home in Dulwich, London; 7 r The home of Ben Johns and Deb Waterman Johns; 8 Madame Sera Hersham-Loftus's home; 9 The Fried family home in London; 10 l Stella's room in NYC; 10 r Glasserman/Gilsanz Residence; 11 The designer Etienne Mery's home in Paris; 12–13 Polly and Bella's rooms in South London; 14–15 Architect & interiors: Nico Rensch, Architeam; 16–17 Madame Sera Hersham-Loftus's home; 18–19 Polly and Bella's rooms in South London; 20–23 Wayne & Gerardine Hemingway of HemingwayDesign's home in Sussex; 24–25 The designer Etienne Mery's home in Paris; 26–27 The Fried family home in London; 28–29 Rose Uniacke's home in London; 30 –31 The designer Etienne Mery's home in Paris; 32 Isabel & Ricardo Ernst's family home; 33 Rose Uniacke's home in London; 34 l The Marsden family home in Dulwich, London; 34 r Rose Uniacke's home in London; 35 Jon Pellicoro Artist and Designer; 36–37 The Fried family home in London; 38–39 Madame Sera Hersham-Loftus's home; 40–41 Freddie Hair's room in London; 42–43 Rose Uniacke's home in London; 44–45 Interior designer Lisa Jackson's home in New York; 46–47 Jon Pellicoro Artist and Designer; 48–49 Isabel & Ricardo Ernst's family home; 50–51 Freddie Hair's room in London; 52–53 Architect & interiors: Nico Rensch, Architeam; 54 Interior architecture; matali crasset; 55 The Marsden family home in Dulwich, London; 56 l The home of Ben Johns and Deb Waterman Johns; 56 r Interior architecture; matali crasset; 57 The Marsden family home in Dulwich, London; 58–59 The O'Connor Bandeen family home in London; 60 al & ar The Eclair-Powell home in London; 60 b The Marsden family home in Dulwich, London; 61 The Eclair-Powell home in London; 62–63 Interior architecture; matali crasset; 64 The Marsden family home in Dulwich, London; 65 l Jon Pellicoro Artist and Designer; 65 r The home of Ben Johns and Deb Waterman Johns; 66–67 The designer Etienne Mery's home in Paris; 68–69 Val, Wim, Kamilla, Juliette and Joseph's home in Ghent; designed and built by Wim Depuydt, Architect; 70l Thomas Siffer and Els Lybeer, Ghent, Architect Wim Depuydt; 70 r Glasserman/ Gilsanz Residence; 71 The O'Connor Bandeen family home in London; 72–73 interior architecture; matali crasset; 74–77 Val, Wim, Kamilla, Juliette and Joseph's home in Ghent; designed and built by Wim Depuydt, Architect; 78–79 Dr Alex Sherman and Ms Ivy Baer Sherman's residence in New York City; Mullman Seidman Architects; 80–81 Jon Pellicoro Artist and Designer; 82–83 Glasserman/Gilsanz Residence; 84–87 The O'Connor Bandeen family home in London; 88 interior architecture; matali crasset; 89 Wayne & Gerardine Hemingway of HemingwayDesign's home in Sussex; 90 l The Marsden family home in Dulwich, London; 90 r The Fried family home in London; 91 Val, Wim, Kamilla, Juliette and Joseph's home in Ghent; designed and built by Wim Depuydt, Architect; 92–93 Wayne & Gerardine Hemingway of HemingwayDesign's home in Sussex; 92 b Isabel & Ricardo Ernst's family home; 94 a Glasserman/Gilsanz Residence; 94 b Val, Wim, Kamilla, Juliette and Joseph's home in Ghent; designed and built by Wim Depuydt, Architect; 95 Polly and Bella's rooms in South London; 96–97 The Marsden family home in Dulwich, London; 98–99 The O'Connor Bandeen family home in London; 100 –101 Wayne & Gerardine Hemingway of HemingwayDesign's home in Sussex; 102 –103 The home of Ben Johns and Deb Waterman Johns; 104 interior architecture; matali crasset; 105 Wayne & Gerardine Hemingway of HerningwayDesign's home in Sussex; 106 The Eclair-Powell home in London; 107 The home of Ben Johns and Deb Waterman Johns; 108 l The Fried family home in London; 108 r The home of Ben Johns and Deb Waterman Johns; 109–111 interior architecture; matali crasset; 112 Rose Uniacke's home in London; 113 The home of Ben Johns and Deb Waterman Johns; 114–117 The Eclair-Powell home in London; 118–119 The home of Ben Johns and Deb Waterman Johns; 120 –121 Isabel & Ricardo Ernst's family home; 122 Stella's room in NYC; 123 The Eclair-Powell home in London; 124 Stella's room in NYC; 125 Val, Wim, Kamilla, Juliette and Joseph's home in Ghent; designed and built by Wim Depuydt, Architect; 126–129 Thomas Siffer and Els Lybeer, Ghent; Architect: Wim Depuydt; 130–131 The designer Etienne Mery's home in Paris; 132–133 Stella's room in NYC; 134–135 Interior designer Lisa Jackson's home in New York; 136–137 Val, Wim, Kamilla, Juliette and Joseph's home in Ghent; designed and built by Wim Depuydt, Architect; 138 -141The Marsden family home in Dulwich, London; 142 a The Eclair-Powell home in London; 142 b interior architecture; matali crasset; 143 Val Wim, Kamilla, Juliette and Joseph's home in Ghent; designed and built by Wim Depuydt, Architect; 144–145 The home of Ben Johns and Deb Waterman Johns; 146–147 The O'Connor Bandeen family home in London; 148 l Wayne & Gerardine Hemingway of HemingwayDesign's home in Sussex; 148 b The Marsden family home in Dulwich, London; 149 Thomas Siffer and Els Lybeer, Ghent; Architect: Wim Depuydt; 150–151 The Marsden family home in Dulwich, London; 152–153 The designer Etienne Mery's home in Paris.

Architects and designers

Architects and designers whose work is featured in this book:

Ben Johns CEO
Scout (Bags and floor coverings) Ltd
1055 Thomas Jefferson Street NW
Washington DC 20007
T: + 202 944 9590
F: + 202 944 9593
ben@bungalowco.com
and
Deb Waterman Johns
Get Dressed Wardrobe and Home & Fifi
1633 29th Street NW
Washington DC 20007
T: + 202 625 6425
F: + 202 338 2858
deb@dogbunny.com
Pages 2–3; 4 r; 7 r; 56 l; 65 r; 102–103; 107; 108 r; 113; 118–119; 144–145.

Andrew Hair
Tapis Vert
T: 020 8678 1408
tapis.vert@virgin.net
Pages 4l; 40–41, 50–51.

Nico Rensch
ARCHITEAM
Campfield House
Powdermill Lane
Battle, East Sussex TN33 0SY
T: +44 1424 775211
nr@architeam.co.uk
www.architeam.co.uk
Pages 14–15; 52–53.

Mullman Seidman Architects
443 Greenwich Street
New York, NY 10013
USA
T: 212 431 0770
F: 212 431 8428
pseidman@mullmanseidman.com

www.mullmanseidman.com
Pages 78–79.

Jon Pellicoro Artist & Designer
jpellicoro@earthlink.net
Pages 35; 46–47; 65 l; 80–81.

James Slade
Cho Slade Architecture
150 Broadway, No. 807
New York, NY 10038
T: + 212 677 6380
F: + 212 677 6330
info@sladearch.com
www.sladearch.com
Pages 5 al; 10r; 70 r; 82–83; 94 a.

Alex Michaelis & Tim Boyd
Michaelis Boyd Associates
9B Ladbroke Grove
London W11 3BD
T: +44 (0)20 7221 1237
F: +44 (0020 7221 0130
info@michaelisboyd.com
www.michaelisboyd.com
Pages 1; 58–59; 71; 84–87; 98–99, 146–147.

HemingwayDesign
www.hemingwaydesign.co.uk
Wallpaper:"4 Walls" by HemingwayDesign for Graham and Brown; Tiles:"Wet Tiles" by HemingwayDesign for British Ceramic Tiles
Pages 20–23; 89; 92–93; 100–101; 105; 148 l.

Lisa Jackson Ltd.
T: + 212 593 0117
LCJPeace@aol.com
Beds: Upholstered beds by Lisa Jackson Ltd
Pages 44–45; 134–135.

Wim Depuydt
Depuydt.architect@pandora.be
T: + 32 495 777 217
Pages 68–70 l; 76–77; 91; 94 b; 125–129; 136–137; 143; 149.

Rose Uniacke Interiors
8 Holbein Place
London SW1W 8NL
T: +44 (0)20 7730 7050
www.roseuniacke.com
Pages 28–29; 33; 34 r; 42–43; 112.

The Marsden family home in Dulwich, London
Designed by Kim Quazi
Acq architects
4 John Prince's Street
London W1G 0JL
T: 020 7491 4272
info@acq-architects.com
Pages 6 l; 34 l; 55; 57; 60 b; 64; 90 l; 96–97; 138–141; 148 b; 150–151.

DesignerEtienne Mery
johngo@club-internet.fr
Pages 5c; 11; 24–25; 30–31; 66–67; 130–131;152–153.

www.baroquegarden.com
Pages 12–13; 18–19; 95.

matali crasset productions
26 rue du buisson saint louis
75010 Paris
France
T: + 33 1 42 40 99 89
F: + 33 1 42 40 99 98
matali.crasset@wanadoo.fr
www.matalicrasset.com
Pages 54; 56 r; 62– 63; 72– 73; 88; 104; 109–111; 142 b.

www.seraoflondon.com
Pages 8; 16–17; 38–39.

The publishers would like to thank the following: Hector and Olive; Luna; Bo, Tucker and Gibson; Bella and Polly; Felix; Laura and Jasmin; Max, Jimmy, Laura, Jessie and Rosalie; Ellie, Rea, Stefan and Matthew.

Index

Figures in italics indicate captions.

Acknowledgments

Teen Zone was born out of my desire to prove that parents and teens can enjoy great design and sociably co-exist. So thank you to Alison Starling and David Peters, and to my agent, Fiona Lindsay of Limelight Management, for backing the idea!

Thank you, Winfried, for taking fresh, relaxed photographs that so perfectly capture the spirit of the book. And thank you to Annabel Morgan for flawless editing, Megan Smith for the funky design and Jess Walton for cool locations.

Thank you to all the families whose homes we invaded, and all the teens and parents whose opinions I canvassed. And a special thanks to Year Nine at Putney High School, for their enthusiastic insider tips on what makes the perfect girl's bedroom.

Thanks to Harry and Ann, my parents, and Sally, my sister, who endured my own teen tip in the design wasteland of the 1970s! And to Anthony, Cicely and Felix, who can't wait to experiment with cool teen spaces at home.